D1133778

ADVANCED PRAYERS THAT SHAKE HEAVEN AND EARTH

By Daniel Duval

Covenant House Publishing LLC

Copyright © 2019 by Daniel Duval

ISBN: 978-1-64633-208-3

DEDICATION

This book is dedicated to my incredible wife, Christian, who is my partner in pursuing the extraordinary. This book is also dedicated to the countless believers that are fighting the good fight of faith and waiting for their upgrade. God has heard our cries and is pouring out solutions that are taking us far beyond our former limitations.

ENDORSEMENTS

Sometimes when we pray it can feel powerless, like aimlessly throwing darts at a dart board. Dan Duval's *Advanced Prayers that Shake Heaven and Earth* book is a vital tool that reveals insight on how to decree out of the Courts of Heaven using different strategies. This book has an amazing collection of prayer resources with real life testimonies. If you desire to have your prayer life go to another level, I highly recommend Dan Duval's *Advanced Prayers that Shake Heaven and Earth* to be a part of your everyday life.

Adam F Thompson

Prophetic ministry and international author

www.voiceoffireministries.org

Daniel Duval unveils a masterful language by which believers can align their faith and spirit to the protocols of the Courts of Heaven for maximum prayer results. Get connected to heaven by using this language!

Hugh Daniel Smith

Senior Pastor, Embassy Covenant Church International

www.hughdanielsmith.com

What a great time to be alive! Things on the earth are changing rapidly, and while it would seem that there is an onslaught of darkness manifesting through each tier of society, God is raising up a standard. I believe that God has a company of people who through the Spirit of Wisdom and Understanding, Counsel and Might, are not just settling for the status quo, but are committed to seeing the convergence of heaven and earth. I believe that Daniel Duval is a significant fore-runner in this mandate.

On several occasions, I have received prayer ministry from Daniel and have found the results to be profound and life changing. While Daniel has faithfully employed tried-and-true heavenly weapons and strategies to see results, I believe that God has also revealed to him wisdom keys that are tailor-made to be effective in the uniqueness of this season.

Don't just purchase this book. Make sure you also diligently apply the strategies, prayer, and wisdom that it carries so you can see the breakthrough and transformation that God has for you in His great love and generosity.

Todd Weatherly
Founder, Field of Dreams Australia
www.fieldofdreams.org.au

The Book of James clearly tells us "...the prayer of a righteous person has great power as it is working. Elijah was a man with a nature like ours and he prayed fervently that it might not rain and for three years and six months it did not rain on the earth. Then he prayed again, and heaven gave rain and the earth bore its fruit" (James 5:16-18 ESV).

A righteous person is one who trusts God at his word and lives in relationship with the Father, in union with the Son, and with empowerment from the Holy Spirit. The church as a Spirit-people are called by God to offer prayers of all kinds. As a royal priesthood, God's Spirit-people are to trust that God hears and responds to our prayers. Jesus, as the Lord of Hosts, dispatches his angels to accomplish the intention of his words in our mouths. Our words, as God's Spirit-people, carry genuine spiritual authority to achieve extraordinary outcomes when prayed with God's faith. Jesus said we can, "speak to our mountains". In other words, Jesus anticipated that those born again of his Spirit would carry spiritual and delegated kingdom authority, through the power of God's words, to continually destroy the works of darkness and establish God's kingdom realm in both the spiritual and physical realms.

Through Daniel's new book, *Advanced Prayers that Shake Heaven and Earth*, the church is equipped and encouraged to become powerful and effective in prayer. Daniel, yet again, does a wonderful job in this resource by placing us in a position to use God's words in a powerful way through prayers of faith. When we understand the power of God's words, and the mechanics of the spiritual realm, we become more confident that our prayers will be effective, and that they carry a clear intention and destination. There is nothing more powerful that having God's Spirit empowering us to pray God's word to accomplish his will and fulfill our destiny and mandate on earth.

This book will become a useful and effective resource for any believer that wants to be guided into more advanced prayer.

Paul Tothill, BA (Hons), BLS (Hons), GCLP
Senior Leader, Gateway Church, Adelaide Australia
www.paultothill.com

Advanced Prayers that Shake Heaven and Earth is truly a pioneering work in its field. This second installment from Daniel is even more profoundly thorough and technical than its predecessor, giving us more tools to help identify and shift structures/strongholds that oppose us walking in victory and abundance.

This book and its predecessor give us much needed insight into the dynamics of prayer, the spirit world, and our mandate to release heaven on Earth. I believe they are both important tools for the equipping of the Body of Christ at this time in history.

Daryl Crawford-Marshall
Daryl Crawford Ministries
www.darylcrawfordministries.com

Prayer is the key element of power in the Christian life. While attending the largest seminary in the world, there were many professors who talked about prayer, but they were mainly "armchair pray-ers." Daniel Duval is an experienced prayer warrior. He learned to pray on the front lines, battling the forces of darkness in spiritual warfare. I have personally talked to numerous people who have been tremendously helped by the specific prayers written by Daniel. I encourage you to use his book *Advanced Prayers that Shake Heaven and Earth*. This book is designed to take Christians to a higher level of victory in their prayer lives than ever before.

Preston T. Bailey, Jr., PhD, D.Min.
www.spiritualwarfarecenter.com

Dan Duval is a cutting-edge pioneer in the art of spiritual warfare. His intimate relationship with God affords him heaven's greatest warfare strategies, and his heart of compassion brings the zeal of the Lord into every prayer. This volume belongs in the library of every minister with the courage to engage the forces of heaven against the adversary. Engage with the complete assurance of victory in the hands of the living God. May the joy of this achievement resonate deeply in your spirit.

Kay Tolman

Revelation Gateway Ministries, LLC

www.rgmconnect.com

As a healing and deliverance ministry, we have seen firsthand the effectiveness of the prayers that Dan has written. The verbiage may sound strange to some, but dark forces recognize the power and accuracy of the commands. We highly recommend these two books of prayers—as well as other books that Dan has written—to all who are serious about setting people free and being sure that the gates of Hades will not prevail against the Ekklesia! Blessing him with more revelation from God's throne!

Barbara Bucklin

Founder and president, Luke 4:18 Ministries

www.luke-418.com

Essential, equipping and primarily foundational! These prayers are a vital and necessary resource for any Christian who needs a deeper dive into greater healing, restoration and breakthrough manifestation in their journey. Let there be no doubt how critical it is to understand the tools boldly presented here. Own it, use it, share it, and move past barriers that have been keeping you from what Father Yahweh has for you! Dig in and partake!

Ruthie Andrews, LPC
Kyrie Counseling
www.kyriecounseling.com

Daniel has the ability to see bondage and then create a prayer that cuts to the heart of the matter to bring about freedom. I appreciate his gifts immensely and as a deliverance and inner healing coach, I use Prayers That Shake Heaven and Earth as a tool all the time. I either use them straight out of the book or modify them for a client's specific issue. When I read *Advanced Prayers That Shake Heaven and Earth*, I could clearly see how Daniel has been shown game-changing legal language for bringing cases into the Courts of Heaven. Because we deal with high-level warfare and need specific, "hits-the-mark" language, this new book may be the nuclear bomb against the kingdom of darkness we've been waiting for. I am excited and very honored to apply these prayers in my ministry. Thank you, Father God, for Daniel and his family!

Dianne Poore

Arcstar Ministries

www.arcstar.org

TABLE OF CONTENTS

INTRODUCTION

Welcome to *Advanced Prayers that Shake Heaven and Earth*. This is a follow-up to *Prayers that Shake Heaven and Earth* and has been assembled to expand the toolbox the first volume only started. This is a book containing a supremely powerful collection of prayers developed to get results! The need is real, and believers all over the world are struggling to achieve a prayer life and personal ministry defined by powerful and consistent results. People have prayed, they have fasted, and they have prayed some more, and are befuddled as to why things haven't shifted the way they'd hoped.

That's why I'm here to help. My name is Daniel Duval and I am the executive director of BRIDE Ministries International, the senior leader of the BRIDE Ministries Church, the creator of the BRIDE Ministries Institute, the host of *Discovering Truth* with Dan Duval, and a coach specializing in helping people find healing and deliverance from highly traumatic backgrounds, including satanic ritual abuse and government-sponsored mind control projects. I have worked with all kinds of individuals, from stay-at-home moms and pastors to Illuminati defectors, trained super-soldiers, and people from long lines of generational witchcraft, just to name a few.

Here's what I've learned. The tools and prayer strategies I started with when I first set out to help people were not effective. In fact, many times, they didn't work at all. I said many heartfelt prayers that yielded no results. My prayers would earn me a polite thank you, and I would watch people walk away unchanged. Sometimes I would get partial results, but this was the exception to the rule. It was a big deal! The idea that there could be prayers that produced anticipatable results felt like good ole mythology. This wasn't a surprise though, because I grew up in churches where the same people had the same set of problems year after year, despite the prayers they received and church services they attended. Nonetheless, I was frustrated. What was I missing?

When I finally began to find approaches, prayers, and strategies that did work, I wrote them down. The more tools I developed, the more our ministry boomed. I published a large collection of prayers to our ministry website that became widely shared around the internet. Then people began to print them out and complain about all the paper and ink that printing the prayers required, not to mention the inconvenience of storing them in a binder. So, I put them all in a book and called it *Prayers that Shake Heaven and*

Earth. We enjoyed a lot of breakthrough testimonies and success stories from the prayers outlined in that book. Even now, the testimonies continue to pour in. However, it wasn't enough. Even as I was putting that book into print, I was in the process of outlining more prayers that I found were necessary in order to solve the incredibly complex bondages from which people were seeking freedom.

This book is the result of my pursuit to outline a collection of the most powerful and effective prayer strategies imaginable. I want people connected with the breakthrough they are believing God for, plain and simple. This book will go far beyond the first volume, providing high-powered prayer resources that are best utilized by a trained practitioner. This is not your basic feel-good prayer book. This is an arsenal of prayer resources that will take you to very deep levels of spiritual mechanics. For this reason, I highly recommend familiarizing yourself with our ministry institute at www.brideministriesinstitute.com. Particularly in the higher-level courses, you will receive the foundation you need in order to grasp some of the language found in these prayers. I will not be explaining the revelation behind the prayers in this volume because *this book is a prayer resource and not a teaching tool.*

Do not be surprised that many of the prayers outline instructions regarding how they are to be used. Can you hurt yourself by engaging haphazardly in some of the prayers in this volume? **Yes.** If you are new to Christianity, I, as the author, do not recommend this book to you at all. Start with *Prayers that Shake Heaven and Earth.* If you are seasoned, trained, and ready for next-level tools that will help you walk out your mandates in Christ, this book is for you. This book is also for you if you have already begun a deliverance and healing journey and find it necessary to work with tools that will allow you to walk free from deep bondages that other prayer strategies have not been able to address.

Having laid this out, it is my prayer that this volume will prove to be extremely helpful for those that are ready for it. It will begin with an explanation of how to be saved, because unless you have put your faith in Jesus Christ, the rest of this book will not do you much good. Then, this book will get right to the meat. May the glorious power of heaven rest upon the words of this volume.

GENERAL PRAYERS

The Lord also will roar from Zion, And
utter His voice from Jerusalem;

The heavens and earth will shake; But the
Lord will be a shelter for His people,

And the strength of the children of Israel.

Joel 3:16

HOW TO BE SAVED

To choose Jesus as our personal Lord and Savior, we must believe that he is the only begotten Son of the Father. When he came to earth, he was born of a virgin, being entirely God and entirely man. He lived among us, being tempted in all points as we are, yet untainted by sin. In this way, he became an acceptable sacrifice for the sins of man. God sent him because he loved the world, and he still does. This means that he loves you, and he sent his Son to lay down his life so he could restore and fulfill yours!

God was burdened with an unquenchable love for the whole world. For this love, Jesus died an excruciating, reprehensible, and utterly denigrating death. He was beaten, and his hairs were plucked from his face. A crown of thorns was twisted around his scalp, rupturing blood vessels so that the blood poured from his head. He was beaten with a cat-o'-nine-tails: a whip with nine strands often containing shards of metal, bone, and glass. The stripes upon his back were not from bruised or bleeding skin. His flesh was voraciously torn from his back, and the muscles and bones were left totally exposed. After the soldiers were finished, the skin and muscle that was still attached to his body hung in ribbons.

Upon this back they laid a cross, forcing him to carry it alone. As he dragged this cross, the weight pressed into his open body, inserting splinters of wood. When he could no longer carry it, the cross was given to another, yet Jesus was forced to walk the remaining distance to Golgotha. He was dehydrated. As he walked, the blood that continually dripped into his eyes caused severe burning, and the flesh of his back was totally exposed. He did this for you!

At Golgotha, where Jesus was crucified, they laid his body upon the cross, naked. They distributed his garments amongst themselves. For all of those who have ever been raped, in this moment, Jesus felt that shame. They nailed him to that cross, placing the nails into the major nerves connecting the hands to the central nervous system. They placed a single nail through both of his feet. His legs were not allowed to hang straight down but were fixed so that his knees were bent at forty-five degrees, causing severe and excruciating cramping in his thighs. His muscles fatigued in minutes, but he continued to live for hours.

Upon the cross, death came by asphyxiation. In the position that Jesus was nailed to the cross, it was impossible to breathe. It was not that he was gasping for air. The position of the crucifixion caused his lungs to be maximally inflated with air. He had to struggle to breathe out. Jesus had to drag his back up and down the wooden cross for hours before breathing his final breath. In order to drag his open flesh up the cross, he had to push up on his feet, causing his hands to twist upon the nails that were driven through his nerves. Crucifixion placed the body in such a position that the joints of the arm would slowly become dislocated as the victim suffered. By the time Jesus neared death, all of his bones were out of joint, adding literal inches to the length of his arms. He did this for you!

With a face marred beyond recognition, Jesus cried out to the Father in Matthew 27:46, "My God! My God! Why have you forsaken me?" He suffered the ultimate feelings of rejection because when he became sin for us, he had to be forsaken by his Father in heaven. In the end, the internal complications resulting from crucifixion ruptured the heart of Jesus. When the soldiers pierced his side, blood and water poured out. Jesus died of a heart broken for us. He died that we might live; not only eternally, but also abundantly. He died to give us the very life of God. He is the acceptable sacrifice—the only sacrifice that God would accept for our sins.

To be saved, we must not only believe that Jesus died, but that he was resurrected on the third day. The victory wasn't in the death, but in the resurrection of Jesus Christ, when he arose having all power in heaven and on earth (Matthew 28:18). He later ascended to heaven and sat down at the right hand of the Father, where he remains to this day, continually making intercession for us. This is the God I serve! This is the God of love! This is the gospel of Jesus Christ! The Bible says that if we confess the Lord Jesus Christ with our mouth and believe in our heart that God has raised him from the dead, we will be saved (Romans 10:9). If you believe this testimony of Jesus Christ in your heart, then you can confess this prayer with your mouth, and you will be saved:

> Jesus, I come before you and acknowledge that I am a sinner. I repent. I call upon your name and I ask you to cleanse me with your blood. Forgive me of my sins. I invite you into my heart, Jesus Christ. I believe that you were born of a virgin, died, and were resurrected on the third day that I might have eternal life. I open my life to you, and I ask you to come in and be my Lord and Savior. Thank you for saving me. Amen.

If you just said that prayer, you now also have eternal life in Christ Jesus. When you die, you will immediately be escorted to heaven to spend eternity with God (2 Corinthians 5:8). In Jesus, you will find a leader that will never fail you. He will right every wrong and heal every wound. Your hope and confidence has just been placed in the greatest Leader the cosmos will ever know.

ENGAGE WITH JESUS PRAYER

Experiencing an encounter with Jesus Christ changes us. We need to understand that we can have encounters with Jesus any time, and on any day! Yes, this may sound foreign to some, but for others, we have already engaged with this as our reality. For some people, an encounter is experienced as a sense of nearness, though they cannot see or hear him. For others, encounters with Jesus are vivid, and they are able to clearly discern what he is doing in the spirit realm. This should come as no surprise since it is written that he will never leave us or forsake us (Hebrews 13:5).

Some people get very religious and assume that encounters with God are reserved for those that have died. If this were true, then why did Jesus appear to John in chapter 1 of the book of Revelation or to Paul on the road to Damascus? Jesus made appearances then, and he is making appearances now. He is on the inside of us, for crying out loud! Why would we be offended at the idea that he wants to reveal himself to us in dreams and visions?

When it comes to inner healing ministry, working with Jesus yields incredible acceleration. This prayer is how I get people connected to Jesus in the context of prayer work. The General Clause is very useful for general circumstances. If the person I am working with is really struggling to connect with Jesus or experiences fake Jesus entities when they try to connect with Jesus, the Fake Jesus Clause will prove to be quite helpful in moving that person past the confusion and into a genuine encounter. It is important to understand that there are a lot of evil spirits that dress up like Jesus to confuse people, especially when dealing with those that come from occult and ritual abuse backgrounds. Sometimes fake Jesuses can also be programmed projections, holograms, or soul-fragments of people the person was abused by. Regardless of the case at hand, this prayer will help.

General Clause

Lord Jesus, I come before you in prayer and declare that you are the ever-present help in time of need. I declare that you are Wonderful, Counselor, Mighty God, Everlasting Father, Prince of Peace. You are High Priest according to the Order of Melchizedek. You are the Lion of the Tribe of Judah. You are the Lamb slain from the foundation of the world, having the seven eyes which are the seven spirits of God. You are the perfect Bridegroom, the bright and Morning Star, and my Advocate with the Father. You are the Good Shepherd, the Alpha and the Omega, the Word made flesh. You are the Son of God and the Son of Man, the Beloved, and the King of kings. You stand at the door and knock, and to him who opens up to you, you will come in and you will sup with him. I determine to engage with you and thank you for being present right now.

Fake Jesus Clause

In advance, I renounce and nullify every hidden document, covenant, contract, agreement, oath, or vow made by me or any part of me including clones, holograms, merfolk, twins, copies, duplicates, replicas, derivatives, walk-ins, parents, spouse(s), or ancestors that work to block, hinder, or confuse my ability to connect with you, to hear you, to see you, to have communion with you, and to have uninhibited encounters with you, King Jesus. I identify every program, holographic projection, and device involved in producing fake and counterfeit experiences with you, or depictions of you, and declare that every bomb, trip wire, or booby trap associated with them is deactivated now. I call them unplugged from all power sources and backup power sources and I speak that all related cords, wires, threads, conduits, and cables are severed by the sword of the Spirit. I declare that all fake and counterfeit images appearing and being identified will be immediately bound and placed in a furnace of fire to be locked into a state of torment and cast out of me while all parts of humanity woven into those counterfeit images are separated and delivered to a place of ministry and safety. I declare that every veil between us is now torn top to bottom. Thank you, King Jesus, for being present with me and the parts of me needing your ministry right now.

WEAPONS OF WARFARE
PRAYER 1

Sometimes we need to let off a furious rebuke against the powers of darkness that are coming against us, our family, our business, or our ministry. When it comes to aggressive prayer, sometimes language fails us. There is so much we want to say and declare against the enemy, but what are the right words? If you find yourself in need of the biblical approach to bullying the devil, look no further! This prayer contains a host of weapons of warfare that have been derived from the text of the Bible itself. The word of God is the sword of the Spirit, and when we read the word of God, we find many, many weapons, which can all be activated as we pray. Happy thrashing!

> Father in heaven, I come before you in the mighty name of Jesus. I praise you for your power and great glory. I declare that your name is Jehovah-Gibbowr (Psalm 24:8), the Lord who is mighty in battle. You are Jehovah-Sabaoth (1 Samuel 1:11), the Lord of hosts. I suit up with the armor of God, the helmet of salvation, the breastplate of righteousness, the belt of truth, my feet, they are shod with the preparation of the gospel

of peace. I take up the shield of faith, which quenches every fiery dart of the wicked one and the sword of the Spirit which is the word of God (Ephesians 6:14–17). I also take up the garments of vengeance and the cloak of zeal (Isaiah 59:17). I surround myself with a smoke screen (Exodus 19:18) acting as a sight and sound barrier against satanic agents, interlopers, and evil spirits. I identify the evil spirits and satanic agents that have taken up assignments against my home, family, business, and economy. I speak that the weapons of my warfare are not carnal but mighty in God to the tearing down of strongholds, the casting down of arguments, and of every high thing which exalts itself against the knowledge of Christ (2 Corinthians 10:4). There are more with us than there are with them (2 Kings 6:16) and I declare that your angels hearken unto the voice of your word (Psalm 103:20).

Therefore, I arm your angelic armies with your word and loose carnage against the enemy that has surrounded me, persecuted me, opposed me, and resisted me. I release arrows, lightnings, hailstones, and coals of fire (Psalm 18:13–14). I scatter the enemies that have gathered themselves against me with famine (Ezekiel 5:16) and devouring storms (Psalm 83:15–17 KJV). I engage the spirits that have assembled from underwater locations and speak a sea quake (Haggai 2:6). I speak that they are trapped in prisons assembled round about them, locking them into pocket realms characterized by dry wind (Jeremiah 4:11). I call for the drying up of the enemy's waters. I release engines of war (Ezekiel 26:9 KJV), weapons of war (1 Samuel 8:12), and instruments of death (Psalm 7:13) upon the agents and devices of darkness in the name of Jesus.

I choose to tread upon serpents and scorpions (Luke 10:19). The evil agents must be smitten by the rod of iron (Revelation 2:26–27). I release the battle-axe of God (Jeremiah 51:20) into the encampments of darkness and target obstacles at their roots. The choirs and harmonies of darkness will suffer at the release of the blast of God (Job 4:9) and the rebuke from the voice of the Most High (2 Samuel 22:14). I am a son of God (John 1:12) and an ambassador of heaven (Ephesians 6:20). I was not put here to suffer bullying at the hands of a defeated kingdom. I spite my enemies and exalt the name Jesus, the name that is above every name, at whose name every knee must bow in heaven and on earth and under the earth (Philippians 2:10).

I set fire to the enemy's strategies with the fiery stream of God (Daniel 7:10). I plant snares and traps on every evil assignment against my life, calling them booby-trapped. Ravenous birds, devour wondrously in the encampments of darkness (Ezekiel 39:4 KJV). Locusts (Exodus 10:4), devour the evil words and curses spoken against me, my house, destiny, business, ministry, and everything under my stewardship. I engage with the heavenly bodies and employ the stars, declaring that just as the stars fought from their courses against Sisera (Judges 5:20), so the stars are deployed in agendas to advance the government of God in heaven and on the earth. I am more than a conqueror in Christ (Romans 8:37). I declare that as I break free of fear, for perfect love casts out fear (1 John 4:18), fear of the day and fear of the night (Deuteronomy 28:66) is overtaking the governments of evil in the spirit realm. Tempest, strike the evil powers and do not relent (Isaiah 29:6). Deep sleep (Isaiah 29:10), overtake the enemies that are fleeing, impaling them in their efforts to escape such that they feel the full impact of their rebuke. I declare portals, wormholes, and escape routes are shut down in every realm, age, timeline, dimension, frequency, vibration, planet, cosmos, constellation, and universe, past, present, and future, to infinity, and from the beginning across eternity. May the warhorses of heaven tread down those that revolt against the name of Jesus Christ and the power of his might. I declare a massive clearing in the spiritual atmosphere and environment of my life and those connected to me and thank you, God Most High, that you came to punish the hosts of the high ones on high and the kings of the earth (Isaiah 24:21). Amen.

WEAPONS OF WARFARE PRAYER 2

There are well over a hundred weapons found in the word of God. For this reason, this prayer serves as a follow-up to the first weapons of warfare prayer. It includes more weapons that can be unleashed as a violent rebuke to the powers of darkness. This prayer is really good for clearing atmospheres of heaviness or darkness. It works to prepare an environment for a worship meeting, or a street corner for evangelism. Whatever your needs, the weapons of warfare are extraordinarily effective. They are also great for going to bat on behalf of your kids. This prayer can also be added to the former prayer if you want to simply ground-and-pound the enemy for an extended period of time. Enjoy!

> Father in heaven, I come before you in the mighty name of Jesus because I have been invited to come boldly before your throne of grace to find mercy and grace to help in time of need (Hebrews 4:16). I resist the oppression that has come against me and my house and lift up a shout of praise (Psalm 100:1). I glorify you and your majesty and declare that there is no one like you. The

name of Jesus is the name above every name, at whose name every knee must bow in heaven and on earth and under the earth (Philippians 2:10). I declare that all evil agents must bow the knee at the mention of his name.

I release chariots of God (Isaiah 66:15) into the midst of enemy encampments mounted against my life, family, business, and calling, in the name of Jesus. I declare that the forces of darkness must be cut down. I smite evil agents with madness, blindness, and confusion of heart (Deuteronomy 28:28). I declare that evil forces will loathe the day they receive assignments against me, for I choose to stand in my identity as a child of the Most High God. May the broom of destruction (Isaiah 14:23) sweep up all the defilement the enemy has planted against my life, including his agents and constructs.

I arm the hosts of heaven (Psalm 59:5) with light-based weaponry that hyper-focuses the light of Jesus (John 1:4–5) upon their targets. Go and punish the hosts of evil. I speak that the breath of God (Isaiah 11:4) strikes the enemy coming in and going out. I declare that evil spirits that are apprehended are force-fed the bread of adversity and the waters of affliction (Isaiah 30:20). I declare that they are smitten with boils (Exodus 9:9–11) and they are pierced through with daggers (Judges 3:16).

I speak that there will remain no safe place for the enemies that take up arms against me. The pursuers will become the pursued as the vengeance of God is engaged on my behalf (Deuteronomy 32:35). I speak that my testimony of injustice is beheld in the courts of heaven and becomes the evidence that unleashes the wrath of God (Psalm 59:13) upon his enemies that destroy my life and the lives of those he loves. At his wrath the earth will tremble, and the nations will not be able to endure his indignation (Jeremiah 10:10).

I declare that all of the areas of my life that are under attack are being re-tuned and harmonized to the frequency of the voice of the Most High God (Psalm 18:13), down to the very genetics that compose my person. I receive winds of refreshing and condemn the evil powers that mount themselves against me to the burning wind (Psalm 11:6). I declare that all of their paths, rivers, highways, wormholes, portals, and star gates, are rigged with snares (Job 18:9), trip wires, and booby traps that are linked to devastating glory bombs. I speak that your angels surround me round about, above and below, and against every dimensional access point in Jesus's name (Psalm 91:11). I thank you for the power of the blood of Jesus (Revelation 12:11), by which I cover every component of my life, family, business, ministry, and destiny. Amen.

GANG STALKING PRAYER

Many people struggle with being pursued and attacked by demons, humans out of body both living and dead, and other entities that are difficult to classify. In some cases, entire teams of human agents are at work against an individual's life. This is especially true when a person comes from a situation where they choose Jesus as opposed to an evil mandate or office they were appointed to by the powers of darkness and/or within their bloodline. Gang stalking in the spirit can be executed by ancestors, both living and dead, and by other cult members, in addition to demons and other entities (such as spirit children, clones, hybrid spirits, synthetic spirits, and composite entities). This prayer will provide you with the language to execute a heavenly court case to shut down the activity.

For those that consider themselves to be targeted individuals, we have found that this prayer is quite effective. Many people believe themselves to be tracked by government agencies, cults, or secret groups with technologies they don't understand. Furthermore, they notice strange vehicles following them from time to time, and odd interactions with people when they are in public. They also track anomalies regarding their technologies, such as phones and computers. If this has been your experience, this prayer will prove to be a blessing, especially if it is prayed on a consistent basis.

Please note that the statements in brackets are for instructional purposes. They are not intended to be read out loud as part of the prayer.

> Father in heaven, I come before you in the mighty name of Jesus Christ and I declare that your word says to come boldly before your throne of grace to find mercy and grace to help in time of need. Lord, I have been pursued by my enemies which lay claim to my life, and I am seeking a judgment in my favor that will empower me to walk out my mandates in Christ Jesus.

> I call for a court to be set and I petition Jesus Christ to provide the angels of the Lord with the coordinates of my enemies which are pursuing me to destroy me, to cause me to turn from your truth, to control me, distract me, or to detour me. I pray that the angels of the Lord would use the net of the Lord, and any other technologies necessary, to capture those that pursue me, for I call them indicted and I summon them into the court

of heaven now in the name of Jesus Christ. [Wait to perceive those that are brought into the court before proceeding.]

I ask that all hidden documents, covenants, contracts, agreements, certificates, oaths, and vows that have been signed by me or any part of me, including what I will henceforth identify as "the group": clones, robots, holograms, merfolk, twins, copies, duplicates, replicas, derivatives, walk-ins, parents, spouse(s), or ancestors, assigning legal rights to those that persecute me, be produced for the court now. I call for them to be weighed in the scales of justice. I invalidate every binding document that has been fraudulently created or established against me based on agreements obtained by me or any part of me or the group under duress. I furthermore invalidate every binding document implicating me or any part of me or the group executed by lying spirits that did not fulfill their end of the bargain. I repent for and renounce the creation of all other documents that are left on behalf of me, my parts, and the group. I now call for the blood of Jesus to stamp every document that has been presented before the court empowering those that pursue and persecute me. I call for them to be nailed to the cross of Jesus Christ and to be burned in his consuming fire.

I call for all of the following elements that have been used as access points to my life in both the natural and the spirit to be presented before the court and subsequently burned with the fire of God: hair, fingernails, blood samples, saliva, other sources of DNA, cursed objects, formulas, fecal matter, urine, evil sacred trees, ritual altars, covenantal rings, heirlooms, voodoo dolls, data packets, umbilical cords, tracking devices, tridents, consent forms, and technologies. I agree to specifically address anything else that you require of me, Holy Spirit, that would otherwise keep me bound to my persecution. Bring to the front of my mind any specific agreements or sins I need to lay down now.

[Speak and verbally lay down any specific issues the Holy Spirit brings to your attention, even if you don't fully understand. Confess, repent for, and renounce everything the Holy Spirit brings up. If God reveals parts (or alternate personalities, for those that have Dissociative Identity Disorder) doing ungodly things, claim them as your humanity, forgive them, repent for their sins, speak over them remission of sins, renounce their works, call them fired from their jobs, and call for the angels of the Lord to escort these parts before Jesus Christ for his redemption and ministry.]

To those that have been summoned into the court, I declare that my season of persecution at your hands is now over. It is written that as a man sows, so shall he reap. It is written that whoever destroys this temple, the Lord will destroy.

In keeping with protocol, I separate human and partially human agents from non-human agents within the court. To the human and partially human agents, I offer up the gospel of Jesus Christ. Jesus Christ is the Son of God and the Creator. He is the firstborn among many brethren. He was born of a virgin, he died for our sins, and was raised again to life on the third day. He has ascended on high where he is seated at the right hand of the Father and ever lives to make intercession for the saints. He is the payment for our sins, and should you choose him, you will be justified freely by grace through the redemption that is found in him. His suffering will atone for your sins. If you do not choose him, you will receive in your own members the judgment for your sins and impropriety. Choose now. I pray, Lord God, that as they make their decisions, your stream of living water flows through the courtroom to separate out humanity from those that exist as composite entities. I pray that your sword would sever devices, demons, blinders, artificial intelligence, programs, holographic technologies, quantum interfaces, and other defilements that would otherwise inhibit a decision for Jesus to be made by those present in the court, thus revealing the true conviction of their humanity and not the instruments of their bondage. Lord, I appeal to you to judge and judge justly, and to have your angels escort those that have not chosen Jesus, and all non-human agents, to the place determined for them, such that they cannot any longer take or receive assignments against me to destroy my life and deviate me from my heavenly mandates. I furthermore establish an automation on my freedom such that every reset and backup program to infinity and across eternity is overcome in accordance with this judgment.

In this, I declare complete freedom and autonomy for my body (respiratory system, digestive system, cardiovascular system, renal system, endocrine system, nervous system, musculoskeletal system, exocrine system, glymphatic system, lymphatic system, immune system, and sexual and reproductive system) soul, spirit, heart, decisions, worship, destiny, offices, business, and relationships. I praise you now for freedom, newness of life, and empowerment from you, Holy Spirit. I thank you for setting me free and I pray that barricades would now be set up preventing all attempts at retaliatory efforts. In doing so, I activate your Word on behalf of my life and the lives of my loved ones. I declare, Lord God, that you are my shield, buckler, rearguard, strong tower, and fortress. I put my trust and faith in you, Lord Jesus. I seal this prayer to a realm of timelessness and anchor it to every realm, age, timeline, dimension, frequency, vibration, planet, cosmos, constellation, and universe, past, present, and future, to infinity, and from the beginning across eternity. Amen.

EAR-RINGING PRAYER

There are millions of people around the world that suffer from ringing in the ears. It has several sources that can vary from one person to the next. It should not be much of a surprise that it does not get resolved in the same way for every person. It can be maddening for the sufferer, and if you have struggled with this problem, my heart goes out to you! What you will find here are a series of clauses that address different aspects of the ear-ringing affliction. These clauses have been derived from the different reasons why we have found peoples' ears to be ringing. Only go through as many clauses as it takes for your ear-ringing to stop. While this prayer hasn't proven to work in all cases, there have been many testimonies of breakthrough that have resulted from this prayer.

If this prayer doesn't stop the symptom of ear-ringing, it is likely because something deeper is going on. If this is you, I would recommend working with a qualified prayer coach that understands soul fragments, deliverance, regions of captivity, and technology, and how they can be woven together in strategies to maintain a person in a state of affliction. There may be an inability to get breakthrough because amnesic walls block the path to the real reasons why you are experiencing symptoms. Most of the people that this prayer hasn't worked for come from a background of satanic ritual abuse and government-sponsored mind control, in my experience. For these people, they may have soul-fragments that are compromised in fancy ways that the language of this prayer does not solve. They may also be targeted individuals that are suffering from high technologies that are physically targeting them from inside or outside of this dimension. In these cases, lasting breakthrough may require a journey of inner healing and deliverance, and in some cases interventions in the physical realm.

Witchcraft Clause

Father in heaven, I identify my ear-ringing and bring this affliction before you. I choose to lean on the finished work of Jesus Christ as my deliverance. I bind and neutralize all hexes, curses, incantations, spells, vexes, smotes, enchantments, and jinxes, and send them back on the heads of the senders, and those they work for and answer to, a hundredfold, by the power of blood of Jesus.

Offering Clause

I offer up my ears, inner ears, brain, gallbladder, kidneys, and all related components of my neural networks as a free-will offering in Christ. I repent for all intentional and unintentional ungodly applications of these components of my body. I receive cleansing for them by the blood of Jesus and your living water. I pray that these parts of my body would receive the outpouring of your heavenly oil of anointing. I bless them in the name of Jesus and call them sanctified. I declare that the attack against my ears will not prevail against the voice of the Most High God, and that I have ears to hear what the Spirit of the Lord is saying. I break all curses upon the hearing and reading of the word of God, that are operational against me, with the blood of Jesus.

Tinnitus Clause

I declare that you are my Healer, King Jesus. By your stripes I was healed, and I declare that the Sun of Righteousness rises in my heart with healing in his wings. I bring my cochlea, inner ear, ear bones, eardrum, kidneys, and gallbladder before you. I receive the healing balm of Gilead upon the physical components of my body that are out of alignment with your kingdom and glory. I speak restoration, healing, and miraculous recovery to my body in accordance with my promises found in Christ Jesus. I receive you as Jehovah-Rapha, and I renounce tinnitus and all of its symptoms in Jesus's name.

Parts Clause

I now identify all parts in me that come from my humanity or the humanity of anyone else that has been programmed to act as or to be part of constructs acting as circuits, receptors, receivers, or antenna arrays associated with the ringing in my ears. I call them all fired from their posts now in the name of Jesus and renounce every document, covenant, contract, agreement, certificate, oath, or vow entitling them to be held in place. I declare that these parts are collected by your heavenly hosts and escorted to third heavenly places for processing. I call for their healing and deliverance in the name of Jesus. I speak that their testimonies of injustice are collected and presented before the courts of heaven. I pray for your righteous judgment, and that your justice would transact liberty in my life, and the lives of those whose parts are represented.

CERN Clause

I renounce my tethering to, overlaying and interfacing with, and all existence as CERN. I also renounce all interface points with my genetics, cells of every type, DNA strands, bone marrow, meridian lines, energy signatures, acupuncture points, anchors, and markers. I address all the powers of darkness associated with CERN, including all related oversouls and quantum technologies, and serve them a bill of divorce. I pull up the hidden documents detailing every covenant, contract, agreement, certificate, oath, and vow entangling me and include all related books of wisdom, books of knowledge, books of philosophy, books of time travel, Freemasonic books, programming books, computational books, and all other evil sacred books, and command that they be stamped with the blood of Jesus. I call for them to be nailed to the cross of Jesus Christ and burned with holy consuming fire. I now call for the judgment of, and disconnection from, all related evil laboratories, military bases, radar facilities, cell towers, antenna arrays, satellites, grids, transmitters, circuitry, nanotech, back doors, front doors, quantum computers, holographic computers, physical, electrical, energetic, or spiritual implants, implicated space-filling curves, and all other technology and unnamed evil facilities involved, in Jesus's name. I break all links established by the technology that powers up the ear-ringing affliction through interface with other targeted individuals. I furthermore break all links established by the technology that powers up the ear-ringing affliction through interface with any broken, traumatized, programmed, or captive parts of my humanity.

Internal Labs Clause

I identify all internal labs, computer rooms, and other evil facilities related to the ringing in my ears. I identify every related back door, backup program, power source, backup power source, bomb, trip wire, and booby trap, past, present, and future, to infinity. I cause them to be consumed in the holy fire of Jesus Christ and totally dissolved. I identify every gate, frequency, barrier, equation, cloaking device, force field, sacred geometry, apex of time, DNA matrix, formula, or defensive protocol that would otherwise guard and protect these evil facilities. I ask you, King Jesus, to unlock, set aside, and completely dismiss with these, right now.

I engage with your word in Isaiah 61:1 which says that you came to open the prison to those who are bound. It is written in John 8:36 that he whom the Son has set free is free indeed. It is written in Isaiah 45:2 that you will break in pieces the gates of brass and cut in two the bars of iron. I pray that you would overshadow these evil facilities, Lord Jesus, as you place me under the shadow of your wings. I release the armies of the Lord, warhorses, and chariots of fire. I pray that every related prison, laboratory, and evil facility would be expunged of all human parts, spirit, soul, and body, and that these parts would be exported through a wormhole to third heavenly places for processing. I call for the indictment of all evil ruling entities overseeing these labs, computer rooms, and evil facilities and call for the heavenly cosmic records detailing their acts of injustice to be presented before the courts of heaven. I pray that these entities would be forced to give an account for wrongs committed and suffer the judgment determined by their actions.

I deed the territory of these facilities over to you, Jesus Christ, and I pray that you would rule over it with your rod of iron. I pray that your angels would destroy these evil facilities, and completely remove them from out of me. I call this work sealed in every realm, age, timeline, dimension, and reality, and in this, consummate destruction upon all related backup programs.

Targeted Individual Clause

I now pray that my brainwave signature would be blocked from all access by their technologies and changed by your frequencies, King Jesus. I pray that there would be a disconnection of my brain and ears that is sealed off by the blood of Jesus. I pray for the establishment of a frequency alternating electromagnetic sphere round about me that creates a barrier so I cannot be found by technology or other targeted individuals searching for my signature. I pray that I would be encased in heavenly gold acting as a Faraday cage blocking all other wave-based and frequency-based attacks in the name of Jesus. I also identify all electronic devices throughout my brain and renounce them. I speak that every gate, frequency, barrier, equation, cloaking device, force field, sacred geometry, apex of time, DNA matrix, formula, or defensive protocol that would protect these devices are now removed. I call for the immediate removal of the devices identified in the name of Jesus. I call for the complete disassembly and removal of all control panels connected to these devices. I seal this work in every realm, age, timeline, dimension, frequency, vibration, planet, cosmos, constellation, and universe, past, present, and future, to infinity, and from the beginning across eternity.

Bio Frequency Clause

I speak regarding any and all programming of the frequencies of my brain, heart, and gut. I pray for the discovery of all parts of my person that have endured such programming, including all parts of my brain, heart, and gut, and call for them to be delivered to the feet of the Lion of the Tribe of Judah for complete healing. I engage the armies of heaven, in whatever numbers necessary, in order to ensure the full execution of this prayer. I renounce all evil frequency programming of my brain, heart, and gut. I pray that the timeline of my brain, heart, and gut would be pulled up and that all events of evil frequency programming would be identified, isolated, and purged with the blood of Jesus. I pray that they would be replaced with godly events and that the timeline of my brain, heart, and gut would be reoriented in accordance with what is written in the books of the Most High God about me. I speak that my brain, heart, and gut now receive reprogramming according to heavenly frequencies by Jesus Christ.

Government Programs Clause

I acknowledge my participation, knowingly or unknowingly, in government programs and renounce my involvement in all government programs related to the ringing in my ears on behalf of me and all of my parts. I call for the sword of the Lord to come down and to completely sever me from these programs and all of their backups to infinity, in Jesus's name.

Cancellation Clause

I call all ear-ringing and related false verdicts coming from any courts of hell, cancelled right now in Jesus's name. Amen.

TERRITORIAL
WARFARE PRAYER

Territorial warfare is something that is essential if we ever expect to see lasting change brought to our communities in the physical realm. We can certainly pray to execute territorial warfare on behalf of any geography of any size, but we won't if we endeavor to use wisdom and prudence. Territorial warfare isn't safe for all believers, plain and simple. I begin this prayer with a strong WARNING for this reason. Haphazardly using this prayer will ensure major problems for you and your loved ones, because the language is extraordinarily effective. If you use the language of this prayer to pick a fight where God has not given you a mandate, it will certainly come with a spanking, and one that may affect not only you but your loved ones, too.

The kingdom of God is the government of God where God is King. In his government, he issues mandates. A mandate is a divine commissioning. The only way to safely do territorial warfare is with the right paperwork in the spirit. Unless you have been commissioned by God to pray for your city, state, or nation in a very aggressive way, I would caution you to limit this prayer to that which is in your metron.

A metron is a sphere of assigned authority. It is written, "We, however, will not boast beyond measure, but within the limits of the sphere [metron] which God appointed us—a sphere [metron] which especially includes you" (2 Corinthians 10:13). In this passage, Paul included the Corinthian church in his metron. This was a reflection of territorial jurisdiction that came by way of assigned authority from heaven. When Paul exercised apostolic authority in Corinth, heaven backed him. However, Paul indicates that he did not have a global metron, but that it had limits. Guess what? Yours will have limits too!

When using this prayer, I have included several terms that you can swap into the underlined spaces. For the majority of those that pick up this volume, I would not recommend venturing beyond home or property, as these will default under our metron. The next step would be to engage this prayer for a church, a piece of ministry property, or a private business. This should be done with the approval of those in leadership. However, for those that are called to city, state, or national intercession, this resource was designed to be deployed at these levels.

Having made this distinction, this prayer has been divided up into two parts. Phase 1 of the prayer is designed to be deployed on behalf of all of the terms that can be applied to this prayer. Phase 2 clauses, due to the language and the nature of the subjects addressed, are best utilized when addressing the city, state, or nation. Therefore, if you are going to be addressing your city, state, or nation with this resource, you will want to use both Phase 1 and Phase 2.

As you work through this prayer template, you will notice a few sections that have been put in brackets. These sections will be judgment calls on behalf of the context that you are deploying these prayers into. In some cases, the bracketed portions will be prayed, but in others, they will not be relevant. In other cases, they will indicate where you insert situation-specific information. Happy praying!

Terms that can be applied to this prayer

Home   Property   Church   Business

City   State   Nation

PHASE 1

Open the Prayer and Establish Agreement

Father God, we thank you that you impart to us authority from on high. Based on that authority, we thank you that we have the grace to shift heaven and earth. Father, we bring this _____ to you and intentionally combine our intercession with the prayers of godly men and women, both past and present, who have prayed for the _____ and region with the same heart and spirit. We also join our prayers with those of the cloud of witnesses and with the prayers of Jesus Christ, who lives to make intercession for us. We join our prayers as incense released before your throne.

Enlisting the Cosmos

We declare that the heavens were made to give you glory and praise. We declare that evil assignments and programs seeded in, or imposed upon the sun, moon, stars, and planets against us or this _____ are excised by the sword of the Lord. Just like the stars from their courses fought against Sisera, we declare that the sun, moon, stars, and planets fight against your enemies and work to advance the influence of your kingdom. We thank you that the creation itself shall be delivered from the bondage of corruption into the glorious liberty of the children of God. Therefore, we declare that our prayers restore the heavenly bodies to their first estate, and that they fight alongside of us in our kingdom assignments in heaven and on the earth.

Gates

We identify the gates of this _____: north, south, east, and west, as well as above and below. We declare that the King of Glory stands in the gates and enters thereby. King of Glory, have your way and direct your armies in this _____. We thank you that the gates of this _____ are occupied by your heavenly hosts and purged of evil occupancy. We establish conflict zones at every gate under the control and dominion of the kingdom of darkness, or that is being contested, until that ground is taken by your armies. We thank you that evil gatekeepers and ungodly occupants are being overtaken and forcefully displaced by your angelic hosts. We decree that there are frequent and fresh angelic dispatches to maintain the territory at the gates of the _____. We decree that the gates of this _____ are now becoming heavenly strongholds that are fortified and weaponized. We call for the Ecclesia to be seated in the gates of this _____ to legislate and judge in the spirit according to our identity in Christ. To this end, we activate the spirits of your children in this _____ that are ready for this assignment. Furthermore, we thank you that confusion is being placed on all evil works going in and out of the _____ and that this tremendously increases the sloppiness of the kingdom of darkness. We praise you that all evil works going through the gates are systematically put under heavy taxation and tracking such that the agendas of the kingdom of darkness are tremendously hindered. We thank you that the gates are being armed and fitted with defensive protocols as they are being occupied by your armies. We thank you that the message of the Gospel of the Kingdom is continually declared and displayed at the gates for all who would receive it. We also declare that the gates are repurposed to allow heavenly traffic into and out of the _____ in Jesus's name.

Foundations

Father, we thank you that the foundations of this _____ are being expunged of evil and secrets. We call secret and hidden iniquity, bloodshed, murder, greed, trafficking, covenants, and defilements extracted by your heavenly hosts. We praise you that assignments and scrolls are being delivered to your people who are qualified and rightly positioned to stand in repentance. We activate that which you have written in your books about this _____ into manifestation. We decree that the foundations of this _____ are seeded with your word, which says, "Our Father who is in heaven, hallowed be your name. Your kingdom come, your will be done on earth as it is in heaven." We decree Isaiah 1, saying, "Therefore the Lord says, The Lord of hosts, the Mighty One of Israel, 'Ah, I will rid Myself of My adversaries, and take vengeance on My enemies. I will turn My hand against you, and thoroughly purge away your dross, and take away all your alloy. I will restore your judges as at the first, And your counselors as at the beginning. Afterward you shall be called the

[_____] of righteousness, the faithful [_____]." Furthermore, we address the constructs built upon the foundations that are faulted by bloodshed, idolatry, extortion, murder, greed, trafficking, and other defilements. We declare your word that when the rains descend and the floods come and the winds blow, a house built on sand will not stand. We thank you that ungodly constructs are destabilized and fully collapsed as they are being confronted with a display of might. We thank you that what can be shaken, will be shaken, so what cannot be shaken will remain. We thank you that veils of secrecy that hide and disguise evil are also being torn down and speak that they cannot be replaced by any duplicates, projections, holograms, backups, clones, or derivatives.

Walls

We thank you, Father, that ungodly walls of division in the _____ have been smote and left in a ruinous heap. Walls between denominations, social class, race, political affiliation, and other lines of division are being addressed. We also address walls between husbands and wives, siblings, and key kingdom relationships that bear kingdom mandates. We decree that artificial walls of separation will no longer abide or be upheld in this _____.

Angels of North, South, East, and West

We speak to the angels of the North, South, East, and West, and we say rise up and be strong in the might of God Most High. We charge you and your realms with the names of God, Jehovah-Jireh, Jehovah-Rapha, Jehovah-Shammah, Jehovah-Nissi, Jehovah-Tsidkenu, Jehovah-Makkedesh, Jehovah-Ra'ah, Jehovah-Shalom, Jehovah-Gibbowr, Jehovah-Elohim, Jehovah-Sabaoth, Jehovah-Issuwz, Jehovah-Hoseenu, El-Shaddai, El-Elyon, El-Olam, El-Roy, Yeshua Ha Mashiach. We release a demand that you occupy your seats of authority and execute the will of the Lord from them. We speak to the North Wind and declare that you will drive away the rains of the enemy to make room for the former and the latter rains of God to overtake his people. We speak that you will create a disagreeable environment in this _____ upon those that oppose our God while bringing abundance to the children of the Most High. We call for the South Winds to bring stillness to calamity and calm to stormy territories. Guide the South Winds by your power, Lord God. We call for the East Winds to smite marine kingdom outposts with sand and dust and dryness, bringing judgment upon evil outposts in the name of Jesus. We call the destructive wind of the wilderness upon the outposts of darkness. We say to the West Wind, bring in showers of living water and rains of refreshment upon the children of the Most High God.

Portals and Star Gates

Father, we thank you that portals, wormholes, and star gates being used by the kingdom of darkness in and around the _____ are being plugged up, sealed with the blood of Jesus and the Holy Spirit. We engage naturally occurring portals with warfare executed by your chariots of fire until the territory is taken and repurposed. We cause the interdimensional pathways of the kingdom of darkness to be tied up in knots, and that all their pathways are confused. We declare that portals, wormholes, and star gates will not be successfully employed in the advance of dark agendas as an alternative to the gates. We thwart their use by a show of force in the name of Jesus.

Borders

Father, we thank you that the borders of the _____ are secured by sentinel angels, sent on assignment to stand watch and guard. We thank you that the borders cannot be moved by the enemy. We thank you that you cause sentinel angels to be established at the borders in ever-increasing numbers daily. We also declare that angels stand at the borders who have access to the heavenly cosmic records and the books of remembrance. We thank you that you cause these records to be read in response to any evil spirits who have responded to a call to aid or provide reinforcement to powers of darkness stationed in this _____. We invalidate the power of all human agreement obtained under duress or coercion and expose their extortion, theft, murder, and other injustices against humanity. We decree that in response to the declaration of their crimes, the armies of heaven are loosed to administrate immediate judgment and punishment. We declare that they are cut asunder and suffer the plundering of their territories and storehouses, in addition to the loss of all imprisoned humanity and reduction of their borders. We thank you that all in the kingdom of darkness who attempt to aid or provide reinforcements to the evil powers in this _____ are judged in this manner.

Ley lines

Father, we thank you that you move to cleanse the ley lines of the _____ from the evil that has moved through them. We declare that ley lines are being purged by the river of your living water mixed with oil of anointing. We call this water laced with the razor of the Lord and the dagger of the Lord so that evil people and systems are simultaneously cut loose from the ley lines as a viable power source. We pray that angels would be given assignments to continuously worship the Lord of hosts in strategic places in the _____ that will cause the ley lines to be powered up with your glory. We pray that your appointed individuals and your heavenly structures and strongholds would begin to be plugged into the ley lines throughout this _____ as they become sufficiently cleansed from all defilement.

Firmament

We call heaven and earth as a witness against the kingdom of darkness. We declare your word, which says that the firmament was created to declare your glory and proclaim your handiwork. Based on its defilement from the first estate, we thank you that your all-consuming fire goes through it and comes out of it. We unlock it from all ungodly power sources, backup power sources, cloaks, barriers, frequencies, sacred geometries, and equations. We declare that it is severed and removed from the global geodesic dome. We thank you that all associated wires and cords are also ripped out. Father, we thank you that military activities being executed against targeted individuals in this _____ from the firmament are severely frustrated. We declare unrelenting judgment against the chemtrail agenda and the corporations that establish and advance it over this region. We call for their defrauding, bankruptcy, and indictment in the name of Jesus. We thank you that you cause trace metals that have been deposited to be purged. We thank you for judgment of not only corporations, but also entities and secret groups involved in geoengineering agendas. We decree that they are severely incapacitated in their ability to continue.

Spiritual Atmosphere

We declare that the spiritual atmosphere is continually made ever increasingly treacherous for the agents of darkness. We decree the increase of angelic encounters by satanic agents attempting to go out of body and astral project, by those doing incantations and rituals, and by those attempting to open portals for the powers of darkness. We declare that the routes and pathways traversed by evil spirits are confused and that this region gives way to a massive influx of encounters with Jesus Christ. We declare that the spirit realm is booby-trapped against those taking evil spiritual assignments against your children and that sabotage overtakes the ministers of darkness in their assignments. We dispatch angels to lay these booby traps throughout this _____ day and night. We take authority over dream realms in this _____ and call for strategic heavenly interventions, particularly in the dreams of those that practice witchcraft and lucid dreaming. We call this _____ a liability for the kingdom of darkness and its agents and declare that the shifting spiritual atmosphere produces conviction, repentance, and renunciation of occult powers, in Jesus's name. We declare that your Holy Spirit was sent to convict the world of sin, righteousness, and judgment.

Contending with Inner Earth

We declare that at the name of Jesus every knee must bow in heaven, and on earth, and under the earth. We speak against the abominations and hybrids that have taken up residence under this _____ and declare that the heaven, even the heavens, are the Lord's, but the earth he has given to the children of men. We employ and loose angels of death to wage war on abominations, hybrids, and ungodly offspring that exist as residents beneath this _____ in Jesus's name. We declare that trading floors are purged by living water. We pray that evil thrones, altars, and ritual sites where power transfers occur and where evil covenants are established are challenged by the armies of the Lord. We declare that community leaders receiving power from this realm are exposed and brought down. We make way for the children of light to receive their inheritance not only on the earth, but in the earth as well, and therefore we purpose to take possession of stolen land in the name of Jesus. In this process we call for justice on behalf of blood that has been shed in the earth, and that judgment is released upon the kingdom of darkness in response to the blood that cries out.

Changing the Frequency

Babylon has become a cage for every foul and hateful bird. We declare that the foul and hateful birds are being expelled from this _____ along with other ungodly animals and we open up this _____ to heavenly birds. We declare that their song of praise shifts the frequency of this _____. We also call forth heavenly load-bearing animals to carry in the blessings and increase of heaven.

Surveyors

We identify all evil surveyors that are being released throughout the _____ in order to assess the situation and discover new strategies of warfare on behalf of the kingdom of darkness. We release angels of the Lord to patrol this _____ and we issue arrest warrants to all surveyors that are discovered without legal documentation and paperwork empowering them to do their work. We speak that they will be immediately apprehended, bound, and subjected to judgment and punishment for trespassing. We furthermore address surveyors having paperwork and declare that their paperwork will be examined and judged on the scales of justice. We oppose surveyors presenting paperwork by appealing to the heavenly mandate for this _____. We contend that their work is in direct opposition to the goals of

Jesus Christ, and thus we call for an active opposition of their surveying and pray for this to be executed by the armies of heaven until the evil surveyors are defeated and blocked from further activity.

Future Generations

We declare the word of the Lord in Jeremiah 1:5, which says that "before we were in our mother's womb you knew us." We speak that all of the days of lives were written in your book when as yet there were none of them. And we oppose agendas to destroy the destiny of future generations by subtracting wealth, inheritance, and success from current generations that are turning from darkness to light. We put angels on assignment to make specific interventions on behalf of those breaking free from the control of generational witchcraft, satanism, illuminism, Freemasonry, and other evil secret societies, declaring that their destiny in Christ overrules the legalities the enemy is claiming as they attack them on behalf of their future generations. We also appeal to the heavenly mandates for future generations in this _____ and speak that there will be key, strategic, and continual interventions in this _____ in order to make a way for future generations to step into their God-ordained assignments.

Timelines

We call for the timelines of this _____ to be pulled up and investigated. We pray that artificially injected pasts that have spoiled or altered the present are discovered and overruled. We command that all disingenuous history, known and unknown, that has led to the empowerment of evil strongholds and reinforcements in this _____ are completely purged by the blood of Jesus. We pray that overlays and insertions of false or satanic timelines with the timelines of this _____ are excised by the sword of the Lord and judged. We pray for their replacement with godly events, so that the present is fundamentally altered in favor of the agendas of the kingdom of God.

Armies of the Dead

We open up suit on behalf of this _____ and its defilement by dead human souls and spirits that have been woven into this _____ through covenants with Death and all other manner of establishing anchors and agreements with their presence. On behalf of this _____, we renounce the presence of the armies of the dead and serve them a bill of divorce. We also call for the soul fragments of the aborted children to be gathered up by the heavenly hosts and unraveled from evil entanglements that reinforce control mechanisms throughout this _____. We call for the presentation of every covenant, contract, agreement, certificate, oath, or vow entangling them with this _____ [and its land, buildings, ley lines, temples of worship, evil corporations, graveyards, hospitals, active covens, and residents]. We call for these agreements to be weighed on the scales of justice, covered with the blood of Jesus, nailed to the cross of Jesus Christ, and burned with holy consuming fire. We issue arrest warrants on the armies of the dead that have taken up occupancy throughout this _____ and appeal to your word in Matthew 10:28, which says do not fear man who is able to destroy the body, but fear God who is able to destroy both soul and body in hell. To those gathered up by the armies of heaven we declare, you are dead. We offer up the gospel of Jesus Christ. Jesus Christ is the Son of God and the Creator. He is the firstborn among many brethren. He was born of a virgin, he died for our sins, and was raised again to life on the third day. He has ascended on high where he is seated at the right hand of the Father and ever lives to make intercession for the saints. He is the payment for our sins, and should you choose him, you will be justified freely by grace through the redemption that is found in him. His suffering will atone for your sins. If you do not choose him, you will receive in your own members the judgment for your sins and impropriety. Choose now. I pray, Lord God, that as they make their decisions, your stream of living water flows through them to separate out humanity from those that exist as composite entities. I pray that your sword would sever devices, demons, blinders, artificial intelligence, programs, holographic technologies, quantum interfaces, and other defilements that would otherwise inhibit a decision for

Jesus to be made by those being addressed, thus revealing the true conviction of their humanity and not the instruments of their bondage. Lord, I appeal to you to judge and judge justly, and to have your angels escort those that have not chosen Jesus to the place determined for them. We thank you, Lord Jesus, for receiving those that choose you. We call for heavenly occupation of all key areas being cleared of dead human souls and spirits and call them kingdom territory subjected to the throne of Jesus Christ and his rod of iron.

Establishing the Prayer

We declare that these prayers are established in a realm of timelessness that interfaces with every realm, age, timeline, and dimension, past, present, and future, to infinity, and from the beginning across eternity. We declare that in this way, no manipulation of time or space will reposition the kingdom of darkness allowing them to minimize their losses. We void their resets and fraudulent and illegal strategies to reassert their positions and declare the advance of the kingdom of God. In this we specifically call out the cosmic interdimensional Kabbalistic tree of life that has its roots in the iniquity birthed in Lucifer and declare your doors will not be opened into this city. We also call all judgments issued in this prayer automated across time and space in the name of Jesus. Amen.

PHASE 2

Open the Prayer and Establish Agreement

Father God, we thank you that you impart to us authority from on high. Based on that authority, we thank you that we have the grace to shift heaven and earth. Father, we bring this city to you and intentionally combine our intercession with the prayers of godly men and women, both past and present, who have prayed for the city and region with the same heart and spirit. We also join our prayers with those of the cloud of witnesses and with the prayers of Jesus Christ, who lives to make intercession for us. We join our prayers as incense released before your throne.

Offices

We thank you that the evil and defiled offices in the _____ are being purged with the blood of Jesus. We thank you for their comprehensive disconnection and severing from evil power being sourced to them from the ley lines. We also stand in repentance for the offices in this _____ and all idolatry, injustice, theft, robbery, extortion, trafficking, and other evil works that have been performed in them. We plead the blood of Jesus and call for remission of sins for the political offices of [insert your list of political offices related to your city, state, or nation, such as mayor, police chief, alderman, governor, district attorney, congressman, prime minister, president, etcetera]. We add all high offices in the mountains of business, education, religion, media, arts, and family. We thank you that occupants are actively receiving promptings to repent. For those that do not or will not repent, we decree exposure, so they are caught in their crimes and evicted from office. We declare that those evicted will be replaced with people you have qualified and assigned. We decree your word in 1 Samuel

2:30 that says you honor those who honor you, but those that despise you will be lightly esteemed. We state your word in Luke 12:3, which says that what is said in secret will be proclaimed on the housetops. We thank you for the reorientation of leadership over the systems in this _____ in Jesus's name.

Evil Sacred Trees

We address the evil sacred trees and the kingdoms and evil bloodlines interfaced with them throughout the region. We arm carpenter angels with battle-axes of God and loose them against the evil sacred trees in the name of Jesus. Even now the ax is laid to the root of the trees. Therefore, every tree which does not bear good fruit is cut down and thrown into the fire. Just as you examined the fig tree and found it to be nothing but leaves, we pray that you would examine the ungodly and sacred trees within this _____ for fruit. We pray that just as you did with the fig tree, Lord Jesus, you would do with the evil and sacred trees, judging them and causing them to wither up and die. We furthermore declare that in this _____, blessed is the man who walks not in the counsel of the ungodly, nor stands in the path of sinners, nor sits in the seat of the scornful, but his delight is in the law of the Lord, and in his law, he meditates day and night. He shall be like a tree planted by the rivers of water, that brings forth its fruit in its season whose leaf shall not wither. Whatever he does shall prosper.

The Waters

We call for the drying up of the enemy's waters throughout this _____, both above and below, in reservoirs, rivers, and swamps. We pray that your river of living water which flows from your throne would displace and replace the enemy's waters throughout this _____. We specifically identify waters in this _____ that have been defiled through the application of human blood, urine, feces, and the ash of human bodies ritually sacrificed or murdered. We overrule this agenda with the power of the blood of Jesus, the living water, and the oil of anointing. We call upon you, Jehovah-Rapha, to heal the waters just as you did in the days of Moses when you healed the waters of Marah. We pull down every veil of secrecy and every capacity for mind control and behavioral modification secured by the kingdom of darkness over the residents of this _____ through this agenda in the name of Jesus. We pray that you would make our waters clear and our rivers to run like oil.

Activation

We call for your children to be raised up and activated as anchors of your government for the revealing of your glory in this _____. We call for the mountains and realms of your children to be activated and for the sons and daughters of God to have their lives brought into alignment with their mandates throughout this _____. We call for the mountains of your children to be superimposed over the mountains of society in this _____ and surrounding regions. We declare on behalf of your children that divine appointments are activated, that success is activated, and that your inheritance in your children is activated into manifestation throughout this _____.

Ancient Wells

We break up the ancient wells in this _____ in the name of Jesus. We call opportunities for wealth and industry that have been strategically hidden now revealed to the children of God. We call blessings attributed to this land according to the books of the Lord to be released and harnessed by the children of light. We determine that hidden resources are discovered. We determine that an open portal to the invention of new technologies is established, and that it is for the benefit of your agendas and not the agendas of the kingdom of darkness. We declare that pipelines of provision that have been established and sealed off are now breaking free to the benefit of your representatives. We excavate places where intentional and unintentional burial of your resources has occurred. We establish interface between the land of this _____ and heaven by calling forth heavenly gold to be poured out over this region in the name of Jesus. We activate hidden value in this land. We also direct all value produced by this interface to be directly stewarded by your children and not the children of darkness.

Weather

We declare that weather systems are being brought under the jurisdiction of the kingdom of God. It is written in Job 37:5, "God thunders marvelously with His voice; He does great things which we cannot comprehend. For He says to the snow, 'Fall on the earth'; Likewise, to the gentle rain and the heavy rain of His strength." We oppose the strategies of darkness to manipulate weather systems and defile earth with witchcraft, technology, and man-made manipulations. We appeal to divine order and call for a recalibration of weather systems over this _____ in the name of Jesus.

Establishing the Prayer

We declare that these prayers are established in a realm of timelessness that interfaces with every realm, age, timeline, and dimension, past, present, and future, to infinity, and from the beginning across eternity. We declare that in this way, no manipulation of time or space will reposition the kingdom of darkness allowing them to minimize their losses. We void their resets and fraudulent and illegal strategies to reassert their positions and declare the advance of the kingdom of God. In this we specifically call out the cosmic interdimensional Kabbalistic tree of life that has its roots in the iniquity birthed in Lucifer and declare your doors will not be opened into this city. We also call all judgments issued in this prayer automated across time and space in the name of Jesus. Amen.

MINISTRY PRAYERS

Oh, that You would rend the heavens! That
You would come down!

That the mountains might shake at
Your presence.

Isaiah 64:1

REMOVAL OF
SPIRITUAL DEVICES

This prayer is for the purpose of addressing spiritual objects because in the course of deliverance or inner healing work, they are often encountered. Spiritual objects can be hooks, gadgets, pieces of technology, implants, wires, computers, and more. They can also be knives, axes, spears, and other weapons that a seer discerns to be lodged in a person's body, soul, or spirit. These objects exist in the spiritual realm but interface with the physical body and can even be the cause of ongoing illness or physiological discomfort. Many of those that have encountered spiritual devices in their ministry have learned that the devices can be quite stubborn and difficult to remove, even after the blood of Jesus and the name of Jesus have been invoked. In order to avoid lengthy battles and multiple prayer sessions in attempting to get these devices removed, this prayer provides incredibly effective language that will help you connect to your breakthrough in Jesus Christ.

> Father in heaven, I come before you in the mighty name of Jesus Christ and identify that there is a [description of what is being identified] device attached to [describe the

area of the body] that needs to be removed. I speak that all of its power sources and backup power sources in every realm, age, timeline, dimension, frequency, vibration, planet, cosmos, constellation, and universe, past, present, and future, to infinity, and from the beginning across eternity, are being presently identified. I speak that they must be unplugged, ruined, and consumed in your holy fire now. I declare that every related document, covenant, contract, agreement, certificate, oath, or vow that exists to permit the maintenance of this device is now brought forth. I call them all stamped with the blood of Jesus, nailed to the cross of Jesus Christ, and burned with holy consuming fire.

I identify all gates related to this device and declare that all pathways to the gates are severed by the sword of the Spirit. I call the gates put to sleep and permanently sealed off with the blood of Jesus. I also sabotage all cosmic regenerator and reinsertion devices and protocols, and call for the removal of every gate, frequency, barrier, equation, cloaking device, force field, sacred geometry, defensive protocol, formula, apex of time, or DNA matrix that would serve to protect that which is being addressed. I call in angels of the Lord that are equipped to remove the device. I cause a heavenly substance to be poured out that will identify to the angels all hidden wires, cables, chips, technologies, components, and hidden things that would hinder prompt removal. I pray that you would have your angels remove the device and dismantle all related systems and portals in the name of Jesus. I declare that this is repeated for every backup program across all time, space, dimension, and reality, such that no reengagement or regeneration program or protocol will be able to engage upon its removal. I pray, Lord Jesus, that you would shift and deactivate all markers and sequences in my person that would allow for a synthetically driven reinsertion of bondage.

I speak life to all flesh attachments in the body and apply healing balm of Gilead, oil of anointing, and the stripes of Jesus to all interface points with the physical body. I call for living water to be poured out to cleanse all residues of the device and speak that the afflicted areas are now being flooded with your liquid love. I now pray that the demonic parties responsible for the insertion of this device would be judged and would receive a hundredfold return for the evil they have perpetrated against me. I release angels with the net of the Lord to apprehend anything that would try to reattach and jump back into another place. I call for anything gathered into the net to be brought immediately into the courts of heaven to be judged for its actions. Thank you for the removal of this demonic device, and the justice that is being meted out in Jesus's name. Amen.

FREEDOM
FROM CONSTELLATIONS

To the surprise of many people, they will find that their DNA is woven into the constellations. This type of bondage is much more common than most would be ready to admit. As constellations are composed of a group of heavenly bodies, this prayer employs unique language that is tailored to secure a rapid break-through from this type of bondage. Simply find the constellation that you are entangled with from this list of 88 constellations and use it in the prayer. This list was obtained from https://starchild.gsfc.nasa.gov/docs/StarChild/questions/88constellations.html and details the 88 constellations that are officially recognized by the National Aeronautics and Space Administration (NASA).

As you prepare to use this prayer, you may be wondering where to start. It is common to have to separate oneself from their star sign. This is espe-cially true if you or your ancestors were into astrol-ogy. Beyond this, bondages to constellations are sometimes revealed in dreams. Certain people have reported constellations manifesting to them from their place in the sky while they were in the deep occult or on drugs. If this is something that has happened to you in the past, you will want to use this prayer for that constellation.

This prayer and the prayers that follow are for deep deliverance. If you find that you cannot finish the prayers on your own, or that in saying the prayers there is very little response, even though you know it is your problem, consider going through them with a seasoned deliverance minister or a team of believers that are trained and equipped to do prayer ministry. This holds true for all the ministry prayers contained in this volume. It is not uncommon for people to find that they are not able to secure a full deliverance on their own, even if they are using the right prayers. With this in mind, please be sure you are in a safe environment before attempting this prayer.

Take note that in Point #2, there are four options. Depending on your current situation, you may find more peace with one option than another. Speak the option that provides you with the most peace. Do not speak all four.

Constellations

Andromeda	Princess of Ethiopia
Antlia	Air pump

Apus	Bird of Paradise
Aquarius	Water bearer
Aquila	Eagle
Ara	Altar
Aries	Ram
Auriga	Charioteer
Bootes	Herdsman
Caelum	Graving tool
Camelopardus	Giraffe
Cancer	Crab
Canes Venatici	Hunting dogs
Canis Major	Big dog
Canis Minor	Little dog
Capricornus	Sea goat
Carina	Keel of Argonauts' ship
Cassiopeia	Queen of Ethiopia
Centaurus	Centaur
Cephus	King of Ethiopia
Cetus	Sea monster (whale)
Chamaeleon	Chameleon

Circinus	Compasses
Columba	Dove
Coma Berenices	Berenice's hair
Corona Australis	Southern crown
Corona Borealis	Northern crown
Corvus	Crow
Crater	Cup
Crux	Cross (southern)
Cygnus	Swan
Delphinus	Porpoise
Dorado	Swordfish
Draco	Dragon
Equuleus	Little horse
Eridanus	River
Fornax	Furnace
Gemini	Twins
Grus	Crane
Hercules	Hercules, son of Zeus
Horologium	Clock
Hydra	Sea serpent
Hydrus	Water snake
Indus	Indian
Lacerta	Lizard
Leo	Lion
Leo Minor	Little lion

Lepus	Hare
Libra	Balance
Lupus	Wolf
Lynx	Lynx
Lyra	Lyre or harp
Mensa	Table mountain
Microscopium	Microscope
Monoceros	Unicorn
Musca	Fly
Norma	Carpenter's Level
Octans	Octant
Ophiuchus	Holder of serpent
Orion	Orion, the hunter
Pavo	Peacock
Pegasus	Pegasus, the winged horse
Perseus	Perseus, hero who saved Andromeda
Phoenix	Phoenix
Pictor	Easel
Pisces	Fishes

Piscis Austrinis	Southern fish
Puppis	Stern of the Argonauts' ship
Pyxis (=Malus)	Compass on the Argonauts' ship
Reticulum	Net
Sagitta	Arrow
Sagittarius	Archer
Scorpius	Scorpion
Sculptor	Sculptor's tools
Scutum	Shield
Serpens	Serpent
Sextans	Sextant
Taurus	Bull
Telescopium	Telescope
Triangulum	Triangle
Triangulum Australe	Southern triangle
Tucana	Toucan
Ursa Major	Big bear
Ursa Minor	Little bear
Vela	Sail of the Argonauts' ship
Virgo	Virgin

Volans	Flying fish
Vulpecula	Fox

1. Father in heaven, I come before you in the mighty name of Jesus Christ and I renounce the _____ constellation and its interface points with my genetics, cells of every type, DNA strands, bone marrow, anchors, and markers. I address all the powers of darkness associated with this constellation, including all related oversouls, and serve them a bill of divorce. I pull up the hidden documents detailing every covenant, contract, agreement, certificate, oath, and vow entangling me and include all related books of wisdom, books of knowledge, books of philosophy, books of time travel, Freemasonic books, and all other evil sacred books, and command that they be stamped with the blood of Jesus. I call for them to be nailed to the cross of Jesus Christ and burned with holy consuming fire.

2. In the name of Jesus, I pray that your heavenly hosts would be put on assignment to discover and apprehend every part belonging to me that is loyal to, affiliated with, or in bondage to the _____ constellation.

    a. I pray that those parts would be escorted before the throne of the Father in heaven to be purged and completely healed and delivered.

    b. I pray that those parts would be escorted

to the feet of the Lion of the Tribe of Judah to be purged and completely healed and delivered.

   c. I pray that those parts would be put to sleep.

   d. I pray that those parts would be fired and sent to wherever the Lord Jesus sends them.

3. I now identify all territory in me occupied by the _____ constellation, including territory in my genetic code, markers, cells of every type, bone marrow, DNA strands, and blood. I furthermore include all territory in my physical body (respiratory system, digestive system, cardiovascular system, renal system, endocrine system, nervous system, musculoskeletal system, exocrine system, glymphatic system, lymphatic system, immune system, and sexual and reproductive system), soul, spirit, heart, decisions, worship, business, destiny, stars, offices, and relationships. I deed the territory over to the kingdom of God and I invite you, Lord Jesus, to take the throne and to rule over this territory with your rod of iron.

4. In the name of Jesus, I now bind all gatekeepers and discover each and every portal access point associated with the _____ constellation and its interface points with my genetics, markers, cells of every type, bone marrow, DNA strands, strongholds, and blood, and all sentient intelligences, along with their

agendas, connected realms, timelines, and all associated counterfeit inheritance.

5. I place the blood of Jesus upon every portal access point in all timelines, every realm, age, and dimension, past, present, and future, to infinity, and from the beginning across eternity, and I seal them with the Holy Spirit. I declare that they are put to sleep and permanently deactivated from this point in time and out of time, forward and backward and in every direction, inside out, upside down, back and forth, reversed, inverted, and vortexed.

6. I take the sword of the Spirit, which is the word of God, and I cut myself free from the _____ constellation. I liberate my genetics, markers, cells of every type, bone marrow, DNA strands, and blood. I sever all sentient intelligences, along with their agendas, related realms, timelines, and counterfeit inheritance, in Jesus's name.

7. I return every form of counterfeit inheritance, inclusive of promised wealth, position, status, calling, ability, power, roots, pride, genetic code, seed, ungodly grafts, ungodly citizenship, and all associated rites of passage, and any other form of counterfeit inheritance, in Jesus's name. I refuse it and sever myself from it, and from this point in time and out of time, forward and backward and in every direction, inside out, upside down, back and forth, reversed, inverted, and vortexed,

I choose to receive my inheritance in Jesus Christ. I also declare your Word in Proverbs 13:22, which says that the wealth of the wicked is stored up for the just. I receive the wealth, freedom, giftings and abilities held hostage by the _____ constellation as a recipient of wealth transfer in Jesus's name. Furthermore, my physical children, and children's children, are an inheritance in Jesus Christ, and I receive them and their redemption in Jesus Christ. I renounce all spirit children and ungodly offspring related to the _____ constellation and undo all quantum entanglements involved in their creation. I command their judgment and the purging of the spaces and realms they occupy (or interface with) by judgment through living water mingled with all-consuming fire.

8. I renounce all ungodly paternal and maternal claims, sponsorships and affiliations, apprenticeships, royal appointments, offices and council appointments associated with the _____ constellation. I pray for an annulling of all associated dedications, ceremonies, and celebrations. In doing so, I now declare reversal upon every ungodly pronouncement and judgment passed against me, my household, offspring, finances, marriage, destiny, mandates, stars, godly scrolls, and every other implicated component of my life, arche, and metron.

9. I now receive a blood transfusion, and new breath of life, from Jesus Christ. In the process, I declare that all _____ circuitry, nanotech, back doors, front doors, side doors, trapdoors, infinite doors, hidden doors, cords, insects, vampiric structures, reset devices, energy-draining devices, implants, wires, cables, chips, computers, chains, programs, backup programs, power sources, backup power sources, anomalous magnetic fields, gravitational manipulations, quantum regenerators, receptors, stardust, robots, embryos, fetuses, holograms, clones, data packets, ungodly grafts, and eggs are destroyed, and that all of their residue is purged with living water.

10. I now take authority over every evil spirit on the inside of me and around me that has been operating due to the _____ constellation and its interface points with my associated genetic code, markers, cells of every type, DNA strands, bone marrow, assignments, and blood. I declare that you are discovered, apprehended, bound, pierced through, and thrust out of me for judgment. I also discover every part that is a composite of genetic components of me and others associated with the constellation and held together by a cord that binds. I declare that the cords are cut, that cords in cords are cut, and that all three-fold cords are cut, and that each part is separated into its components. All ungodly components,

and components that are not of me, are now bound. I declare that all of you are now being sent to where the true Lord Jesus Christ sends you.

11. I pray that every spiritual object, tattoo, device, label, jewel, amulet, necklace, earring, rock, crown, ring, bracelet, charm, garment, scepter, marker, power source, tracking device, system, grid, or branding placed in or around every part of me in order to anchor me to the _____ constellation would be consumed in the holy fire of Jesus Christ and totally dissolved.

12. I call for every algorithm or formula created from my DNA and genetic material that is projected throughout the _____ constellation to be shut down in every age, realm, dimension, and timeline past, present, and future, to infinity. I command the immediate apprehension of every cosmic artificial intelligence and technology behind those projections and call for viruses encoded with heavenly algorithms to be uploaded into them and their computers in order to destroy them in judgment.

13. I identify every intergalactic and interplanetary data bank and computer that contains within its records or mainframe: data, equations, parts, algorithms, and information of any manner extracted from my humanity. I declare that angels are sent forth to liberate every part of me

held captive in these data banks. I pray that all other records and information in them related to me would be forcefully erased and permanently deleted. I call for the lightning of God to destroy every ungodly altar (both sacrificial and honorary), as well as effigies contained within _____ representing me or bearing my name, image, or likeness, or in me, representing _____ and bearing its name, image, or likeness. I also call for the annulling and removal of every curse and ungodly insertion placed on the times and seasons of my life in synchronicity with the _____ constellation. I receive synchronization with what has been written about me in the books of the Most High God.

14. Lastly, I stand in my authority as a witness to cosmic injustice and as a child of the Most High God. It is written that the earnest expectation of the creation eagerly waits for the revealing of the sons of God. For the creation was subjected to futility, not willingly, but because of him who subjected it in hope; because the creation itself will be delivered from the bondage of corruption into the glorious liberty of the children of God. Therefore, I call for the purging and healing of the heavenly bodies associated with the _____ constellation with the river of living water flowing from the throne of God. I pray that your lightning would now strike and sever any ungodly points of connectivity that remain. I render this entire

confession established in every timeline, age, realm, dimension, frequency, vibration, planet, cosmos, constellation, and universe, past, present, and future, to infinity, and from the beginning across eternity. Amen.

FREEDOM FROM
EARTH SYSTEMS

It can be difficult to explain to people why they will find that their DNA is woven into earth systems. As you will see, this includes geographical locations, corporations, secret societies, mountains, valleys, and even extends to jet streams, bodies of water, and up and into specific planets. This phenomenon has to do with human design and the nature of the creation. To explore this concept from a theological perspective, I will direct you to work through our BRIDE Ministries Institute Course called *Realms and Dimensions Unsealed* at www.brideministriesinstitute.com. This prayer employs unique language that is tailored to secure a rapid breakthrough from this type of bondage. Believe it or not, this prayer is one of the most commonly used resources I deploy in my personal ministry because of its wide application.

This prayer is especially helpful for those that have received trauma in different locations. It follows that this prayer is extremely helpful for those that have PTSD for various reasons. If there was a battle that occurred that was highly traumatic for a soldier, using this prayer for the location of that battle will be very powerful and bring a great deal of freedom. If a person was highly abused in a childhood home, or in a certain campsite, religious building, or school, using this prayer for that location will prove to be extremely helpful. If a person was a police officer, firefighter, or emergency medical responder investigating a traumatic scene, again, this prayer will be extraordinarily powerful. This prayer applies to ritual sites, programming sites, and secret government installations where ungodly activities occur.

Some people that are involved in the very deep levels of the occult will find themselves in bondage to jet streams, areas of earth's atmosphere, certain metals or elements, and components of Hollow Earth. While the average person may be left scratching their head and wondering if this could possibly be real, I testify to you as the author of this work that there is not a single item listed below that I have not witnessed someone set free from with the use of this prayer. Again, this prayer has become one of my most often used prayers because it has so many applications. As you begin to utilize it, the Holy Spirit will give you wisdom. The lists below will have general words, such as *paths, lakes,* and *mountains.* When using this prayer, it will be up to you to detail which path, mountain, etcetera, you are referring to. For instance, you won't just say "lakes" when you use the prayer, but if you had a near-death experience at Lake

Huron, for example, you would use "Lake Huron" throughout the prayer.

The lists below are broken up into categories to give you some insight into all the ways to apply this prayer. Keep in mind that many of these lists will seem strange. Something doesn't have to be bad for a person to be entangled with it in an ungodly way. Many of the items on these lists are good. What is not good is the way people have been entangled through the spirit in ungodly ways. Let the Holy Spirit be your guide as you work through the lists below, whether it is for yourself or individuals that the Lord has called you to help.

Take note that in Point #2, there are four options. Depending on your current situation, you may find more peace with one option than another. Speak the option that provides you with the most peace. Do not speak all four.

Lists

Geographic Realms: Canyons, Continents, Earth Crust, Earth Mantle, Fields, Mountains, Paths, Roads, Ritual Sites, Sacrifice Sites, Tectonic Plates, Soil, Trails, Valleys, Volcanos, Mounds

Atmospheric Realms: South Wind, North Wind, East Wind, West Wind, Chemtrails, Hydrosphere,

Geosphere, Biosphere, Cryosphere, Atmosphere, Jet Streams, Clouds

Nature Realms: Gravel, Quarries, Forests, Rocks, Mines, Flowers, State Parks, Elements of the Periodic Table, Chemicals, Stones, Plants, Wood, Trees (especially Evil Sacred Trees)

Water Realms: Oceans, Seas, Rivers, Lakes, Creeks, Ponds, Waterfalls, other Bodies of Water (even on other planets), Cities Under the Sea

Regional Realms: Towns, Villages, Cities, Counties, States, Nations, Districts, Municipalities

Energy Grids: Ley Lines, Tropic of Cancer, Tropic of Capricorn, Fault Lines, Degrees of Longitude, Degrees of Latitude, North Pole, South Pole

Hollow Earth: Hollow Earth Sun, Hollow Earth Continents, Hollow Earth Water Systems, Hollow Earth Corporations, Hollow Earth Transportation Systems, Hollow Earth Forests, Hollow Earth Trees, Hollow Earth Animals, Hollow Earth Weather Systems

Revered Structures: Big Ben, Eiffel Tower, Twin Towers, Kremlin, Great Wall of China, CERN, Great Pyramid, White House, Capitol Building, Pentagon, Sphinx, Temple Mount, Altars, Statues, and countless more

Normal Structures: Houses, Barns, Churches, Mosques, Temples, Synagogues, Community Centers, Masonic Lodges, Military Bases, Laboratories, Deep Underground Military Bases, Universities, Schools, and many more

Animal Kingdom: Reptile Kingdom, Amphibian Kingdom, Insect Kingdom, Aquatic Kingdom, Mammalian Kingdom, Bird Kingdom, Livestock, Worms, Maggots, Vermin, and many other kingdoms and groupings

Forces of Nature: Electromagnetic Spectrum, Gravity, Nuclear Strong Force, Nuclear Weak Force, the 5th Force of Nature

Planets: Mercury, Venus, Mars, Jupiter, Saturn, Uranus, Neptune, Pluto, Planet X, Maldek, other planets in other solar systems

Trade: Gold, Silver, Ore, Platinum, Jewels, Various Currencies, Jewelry, Precious Stones, Semi-precious Stones, Human Trafficking, Drug Trafficking, Gemstones, Minerals, Monetary Systems, Central Banks, Banks, Leathers, Furs, Artifacts

Industries: Pornographic Industry, Pharmaceutical Industry, Military Industrial Complex, Landscaping, Hardscaping, Evil Corporations, Oil Industry, Mining Industry, and many more

Government Agencies: CIA, FBI, DOJ, DARPA, KGB, MI6, MOSSAD, and other government and intelligence agencies around the world

Occult Groups and Secret Societies: Freemasonry, Eastern Star, Rosicrucian, Ordo Templis Orientis, Skull and Bones, Hermetic Order of the Golden Dawn, Satanism, Knights Templar, The Bilderberg Group, The Priory of Sion, Jesuit Order, and many more

Technological Kingdom: Screens, Wireless Networks, 5G, EMF, Computers, Cell Phones, and many more

Human Substance: Carcasses, Bones, DNA, Sinew, Bodily Fluids, Abortion Remains, Bodily Systems

Miscellaneous: Idols, Hieroglyphs, Symbols, Vaults, Doors, Windows, Evil Hand Signs, Safes, Cages, and anything else the Holy Spirit would reveal

The Prayer

1. Father in heaven, I come before you in the mighty name of Jesus Christ and I renounce my tethering to, overlaying and interfacing with, and all existence as _____. I also renounce all interface points with my genetics, cells of every type, DNA strands, bone marrow, meridian lines, energy signatures, acupuncture points, anchors, and markers. I

address all the powers of darkness associated with _____, including all related oversouls and quantum technologies, and serve them a bill of divorce. I pull up the hidden documents detailing every covenant, contract, agreement, certificate, oath, and vow entangling me and include all related books of wisdom, books of knowledge, books of philosophy, books of time travel, Freemasonic books, programming books, computational books, and all other evil sacred books, and command that they be stamped with the blood of Jesus. I call for them to be nailed to the cross of Jesus Christ and burned with holy consuming fire.

2. In the name of Jesus, I pray that your heavenly hosts would be put on assignment to discover and apprehend every part, energy center, or gate belonging to me that is loyal to, affiliated with, or in bondage to _____.

   a. I pray that those parts would be escorted before the throne of the Father in heaven to be purged and completely healed and delivered.

   b. I pray that those parts would be escorted to the feet of the Lion of the Tribe of Judah to be purged and completely healed and delivered.

   c. I pray that those parts would be put to sleep.

   d. I pray that those parts would be fired and sent to wherever the Lord Jesus sends them.

3. I now identify all territory in me occupied by
_____, including territory in my
genetic code, anchors, markers, cells of every
type, bone marrow, meridian lines, energy
signatures, acupuncture points, DNA strands,
and blood. I furthermore include all territory
in my physical body (respiratory system,
digestive system, cardiovascular system,
renal system, endocrine system, nervous
system, musculoskeletal system, exocrine
system, glymphatic system, lymphatic
system, immune system, and my sexual and
reproductive system), all portions of my brain
(prefrontal cortex, frontal lobe, temporal lobe,
parietal lobe, occipital lobe, brain stem, corpus
collosum, HPA axis), soul, spirit, implants,
heart, decisions, worship, business, ministry,
destiny, stars, offices, temple, subatomic
particles, and relationships. I deed the territory
over to the kingdom of God and I invite you,
Lord Jesus, to take the throne and to rule over
this territory with your rod of iron.

4. In the name of Jesus, I now bind all gatekeepers
and discover each and every portal access
point associated with _____ and
its interface points with my genetics, markers,
cells of every type, meridian lines, energy
signatures, acupuncture points, bone marrow,
DNA strands, strongholds, and blood, and
all sentient intelligences, along with their

agendas, connected realms, timelines, and all associated counterfeit inheritance.

5. I place the blood of Jesus upon every portal access point in all timelines, every realm, age, and dimension, past, present, and future, to infinity, and from the beginning across eternity, including all alternate earths, and I seal them with the Holy Spirit. I declare that they are put to sleep and permanently deactivated from this point in time and out of time, forward and backward and in every direction, inside out, upside down, back and forth, reversed, inverted, and vortexed.

6. I take the sword of the Spirit, which is the word of God, and I cut myself free from all ungodly tethers to, interfaces and overlays with, and existence as _____. I liberate my genetics, markers, cells of every type, bone marrow, meridian lines, energy signatures, acupuncture points, DNA strands, and blood. I sever all sentient intelligences, along with their agendas, related realms, timelines, and counterfeit inheritance, in Jesus's name.

7. I return every form of counterfeit inheritance associated with _____, inclusive of promised wealth, reward, position, status, calling, ability, power, roots, pride, genetic code, anything lying dormant, ungodly structures, ungodly grafts, counterfeit citizenship, ungodly citizenship, and all associated rites of passage, and any other form

of counterfeit inheritance, in Jesus's name. I refuse it and sever myself from it, and from this point in time and out of time, forward and backward and in every direction, inside out, upside down, back and forth, reversed, inverted, and vortexed, I choose to receive my inheritance in Jesus Christ. I also declare your Word in Proverbs 13:22, which says that the wealth of the wicked is stored up for the just. I receive the wealth, freedom, giftings and abilities held hostage by _____ as a recipient of wealth transfer in Jesus's name. Furthermore, my physical children, and children's children, are an inheritance in Jesus Christ, and I receive them and their redemption in Jesus Christ, and renounce all of their debts to _____. I renounce all spirit children and ungodly offspring related to _____ and undo all quantum entanglements involved in their creation. I command their judgment and the purging of the spaces and realms they occupy (or interface with) by judgment through living water mingled with all-consuming fire.

8. I renounce all ungodly paternal and maternal claims, sponsorships and affiliations, apprenticeships, royal appointments, marriage ceremonies, offices and council appointments associated with _____. I pray for an annulling of all associated dedications, ceremonies, and celebrations. In doing so, I now declare reversal upon every ungodly

pronouncement and judgment passed against me, my household, offspring, finances, marriage, destiny, mandates, stars, godly scrolls, and every other implicated component of my life, arche, and metron.

9. I now receive a blood transfusion, and new breath of life, from Jesus Christ. In the process, I declare that all _____ circuitry, nanotech, back doors, front doors, side doors, trapdoors, inner doors, outer doors, ancient of days doors, infinite doors, hidden doors, cords, insects, vampiric structures, reset devices, energy-draining devices, implants, wires, cables, chips, computers, chains, programs, backup programs, power sources, backup power sources, anomalous magnetic fields, gravitational manipulations, quantum regenerators, receptors, stardust, parallel timelines, counterfeit timelines, time warps, black holes, boxes, tesseracts, counterfeit galaxies, counterfeit constellations, counterfeit solar systems, counterfeit cosmoses, counterfeit universes, counterfeit heavens, robots, embryos, fetuses, holograms, spiral staircases, amulets, clones, data packets, ungodly grafts, and eggs are destroyed, and that all of their residue is purged with living water. I call back all of my DNA that was sold, traded, given away, or exchanged and housed in clones, machines, technologies, entities, banks, and anything else illegitimately possessing it and call for it to be cleansed and

healed with living water.

10. I now take authority over every evil spirit on the inside of me and around me that has been operating due to _____ and its interface points with my associated genetic code, anchors, markers, cells of every type, meridian lines, energy signatures, acupuncture points, DNA strands, bone marrow, assignments, and blood. I declare that you are discovered, apprehended, bound, pierced through, and thrust out of me for judgment. I also discover every part that is a composite of genetic components of me and others associated with _____ and held together by a cord that binds. I declare that the cords are cut, that cords in cords are cut, and that all three-fold cords are cut, and that each part is separated into its components. All ungodly components, and components that are not of me, are now bound. I declare that all of them are now being sent to where the true Lord Jesus Christ sends them.

11. I pray that every spiritual object, tattoo, device, label, jewel, amulet, necklace, earring, rock, crown, ring, bracelet, charm, garment, scepter, marker, power source, tracking device, system, grid, branding, satanic scroll, New World Order scroll, super-soldier scroll, Illuminati scroll, and all matrixes associated with any and all evil sacred orders placed in or around every part of me in order to anchor me to

_____ would be consumed in the holy fire of Jesus Christ and totally dissolved.

12. I call for every algorithm or formula created from my DNA and genetic material that is projected throughout _____ to be shut down in every age, realm, dimension, and timeline, past, present and future, to infinity, including all alternate earths. I command the immediate apprehension of all hybrids and every cosmic artificial intelligence and technology behind those projections and call for viruses encoded with heavenly algorithms to be uploaded into them and their computers in order to destroy them in judgment.

13. I identify every intergalactic and interplanetary data bank and computer that contains within its records or mainframe: data, equations, parts, algorithms, and information of any manner extracted from my humanity. I declare that angels are sent forth to liberate every part of me held captive in these data banks. I pray that all other records and information in them related to me would be forcefully erased and permanently deleted. I call for the lightning of God to destroy every ungodly altar (both sacrificial and honorary), as well as effigies contained within _____ representing me or bearing my name, image, or likeness, or in me, representing _____ and bearing its name, image, or likeness. I also call for the annulling

and removal of every curse and ungodly insertion placed on the times and seasons of my life in synchronicity with _____.
I receive synchronization with what has been written about me in the books of the Most High God.

14. Lastly, I stand in my authority as a witness to cosmic injustice and as a child of the Most High God. I pray that your lightning would now strike and sever any ungodly points of connectivity and demonic manipulation that remain between me and _____.
I appeal to the heavenly mandate for _____. I call for the purging and healing of any redemptive aspects of _____ to be executed by the river of living water flowing from the throne of God. I speak that your kingdom come, and your will be done on earth as it is in heaven, and that your will manifests as a superimposition upon _____. I demand that you administrate justice and judgment in accordance with your wisdom, Lord God. I furthermore claim all godly inheritance and rights that I have been appointed relative to _____. I render this entire confession established in every timeline, age, realm, dimension, frequency, vibration, planet, cosmos, constellation, and universe, past, present, and future, to infinity, and from the beginning across eternity. Amen.

FREEDOM FROM THE KABBALAH TREE

The Kabbalah Tree has been articulated by Jewish mysticism. It contains what is believed to be the pattern for man, as well as for the design of the creation. Unfortunately, many people that have been through occult rituals based on Jewish mysticism or programmed by secret societies that lean on Kabbalah such as Freemasonry, have been programmed with the Kabbalah Tree. This means that they need to be set free and delivered from it. To make matters worse, we found that there is an interdimensional cosmic Kabbalistic tree of life that has its origin in the iniquity birthed in Lucifer. Quite a mouthful, right? This was a massive breakthrough that took us over a year to figure out.

For anyone defecting from high levels of the occult world, they will need to be untethered from the cosmic Kabbalistic tree of life because as long as they are tangled with it, the enemy maintains a hidden back door to reinstate bondage, even as the person continues to pursue repentance, renunciation, and right living. On a traditional Kabbalistic tree, one will find 10 points. Da'at is known to be the hidden 11th point, but we have found that there are 13 points. We were not able to discover proper Hebrew names for them, but in the course of deliverance work, landed on the "occiput interface" and the "counterfeit New Jerusalem" with the help of the Holy Spirit. The fruit of this prayer will be extraordinary. Just be prepared that things may get intense. It is highly recommended that this prayer be used in partnership with a trained prayer minister.

Below you will find a generic picture of the Kabbalah tree and how it interfaces with a human body. There are pictures with much greater detail that can be found on the internet and throughout various types of literature, revealing much deeper revelation into the cosmology attached to this belief system. But to keep this book as straightforward as possible, the picture only reveals the names of the points (sephiroth). Also, note that on a more detailed tree, the points Hod and Netzach land on the hips and elbows, not at the hands, which this representation may suggest.

Take note that in Point #2 of the prayer, there are four options. Depending on your current situation, you may find more peace with one option than another. Speak the option that provides you with the most peace. Do not speak all four.

The Kabbalah Tree and the Design of Man

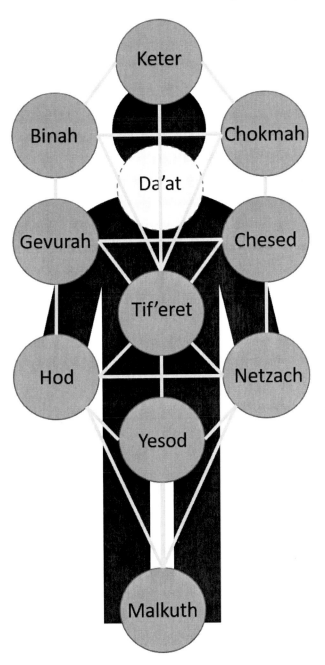

The 13 Points

Keter/ Crown	Binah/ Understanding
Chesed/ Mercy	Tif'eret/ Beauty
Yesod/ Foundation	Malkhut/ Kingdom
(Counterfeit New Jerusalem)	
Chokmah/ Wisdom	Gevurah/ Judgment
Hod/ Glory	Netzach/ Victory
Da'at/ Knowledge	(Occiput Interface)

The Prayer

1. Father in heaven, I come before you in the mighty name of Jesus Christ and I renounce my tethering to, overlaying and interfacing with, and all existence as _____ and all portals that are _____, including all related gates, paths, channels, counterfeit names of God, evil and counterfeit archangels, evil and counterfeit angelic orders, evil and counterfeit planetary forces, and evil and counterfeit living letters. I also renounce all interface points with my genetics, cells of every type, DNA strands, bone marrow, meridian lines, chakras, energy signatures, acupuncture points, anchors, and markers. I

address all the powers of darkness associated with _____, including all related oversouls and quantum technologies, and serve them a bill of divorce. I pull up the hidden documents detailing every covenant, contract, agreement, certificate, oath, and vow entangling me and include all related books of wisdom, books of knowledge, books of philosophy, books of time travel, Freemasonic books, programming books, computational books, Keys of Solomon, counterfeit Tables of Moses, genealogies of Cain, sacred texts of the Library of Alexandria and Vatican Library, and all other evil sacred books, and command that they be stamped with the blood of Jesus. I call for them to be nailed to the cross of Jesus Christ and burned with holy consuming fire.

2. In the name of Jesus, I pray that your heavenly hosts would be put on assignment to discover and apprehend every part belonging to me that is loyal to, affiliated with, or in bondage to _____.

   a. I pray that those parts would be escorted before the throne of the Father in heaven to be purged and completely healed and delivered.

   b. I pray that those parts would be escorted to the feet of the Lion of the Tribe of Judah to be purged and completely healed and delivered.

   c. I pray that those parts would be put to sleep.

    d. I pray that those parts would be fired and sent to wherever the Lord Jesus sends them.

3. I now identify all territory in me occupied by _____, including territory in my genetic code, markers, cells of every type, bone marrow, meridian lines, chakras, energy signatures, acupuncture points, DNA strands, and blood. I furthermore include all territory in my physical body (respiratory system, digestive system, cardiovascular system, renal system, endocrine system, nervous system, musculoskeletal system, exocrine system, glymphatic system, lymphatic system, immune system, sexual and reproductive system, and interstitia), all portions of my brain (prefrontal cortex, frontal lobe, temporal lobe, parietal lobe, occipital lobe, brain stem, corpus collosum, amygdala, hippocampus, HPA axis), soul, spirit, implants, heart, decisions, worship, business, destiny, stars, offices, temple, subatomic particles, ministry, and relationships. I deed the territory over to the kingdom of God and I invite you, Lord Jesus, to take the throne and to rule over this territory with your rod of iron.

4. In the name of Jesus, I now bind all gatekeepers and discover each and every portal access point associated with _____ and its interface points with my genetics, markers, cells of every type, meridian lines, chakras,

energy signatures, acupuncture points, bone marrow, DNA strands, strongholds, blood, and all sentient intelligences, along with their agendas, connected realms, timelines, frequencies, vibrations, and all associated counterfeit inheritance.

5. I place the blood of Jesus upon every portal access point in all timelines, every realm, age, frequency, vibration, and dimension, past, present, and future, to infinity, and from the beginning across eternity, including all alternate and counterfeit creations, and I seal them with the Holy Spirit. I declare that they are put to sleep and permanently deactivated from this point in time and out of time, forward and backward and in every direction, inside out, upside down, back and forth, reversed, inverted, and vortexed.

6. I take the sword of the Spirit, which is the word of God, and I cut myself free from all ungodly tethers to, interfaces and overlays with, and all existence as _____ and all related satanic/Luciferian antiquities and iniquity. I also sever all paths, portals, frequencies, vibrations, gates, rivers, and light connecting my internal _____ to any and all points in the cosmic Kabbalistic tree of life and its related or derived realms. I call for the immediate apprehension and punishment of all entities traversing these paths, portals, frequencies, vibrations, gates, rivers, and light.

I call the work sealed off and cauterized by the blood of Jesus. I liberate my genetics, markers, cells of every type, bone marrow, meridian lines, energy signatures, acupuncture points, DNA strands, and blood. I deactivate my related chakra points. I sever all sentient intelligences, along with their agendas, related realms, timelines, and counterfeit inheritances, in Jesus's name.

7. I return every form of counterfeit inheritance associated with _____, inclusive of promised wealth, reward, position, status, calling, ability, power, roots, pride, genetic code, anything lying dormant, ungodly structures, ungodly grafts, counterfeit citizenship, ungodly citizenship, and all associated rites of passage, and any other form of counterfeit inheritance, in Jesus's name. I refuse it and sever myself from it, and from this point in time and out of time, forward and backward and in every direction, inside out, upside down, back and forth, reversed, inverted, and vortexed, I choose to receive my inheritance in Jesus Christ. I also declare your Word in Proverbs 13:22, which says that the wealth of the wicked is stored up for the just. I receive the wealth, freedom, giftings, and abilities held hostage by _____ as a recipient of wealth transfer in Jesus's name. Furthermore, my physical children, and children's children, are an inheritance in Jesus Christ, and I receive them and their

redemption in Jesus Christ, and renounce all of their debts to _____. I renounce all spirit children and ungodly offspring related to _____ and undo all quantum entanglements involved in their creation. I command their judgment and the purging of the spaces and realms they occupy (or interface with) by judgment through living water mingled with all-consuming fire.

8. I renounce all ungodly paternal and maternal claims, sponsorships and affiliations, apprenticeships, royal appointments, marriage ceremonies, offices and council appointments, and oneness with all persons and entities associated with _____. I pray for an annulling of all associated dedications, ceremonies, and celebrations. In doing so, I now declare reversal upon every ungodly pronouncement and judgment passed against my spirit, soul, and body, my household, offspring, finances, marriage, destiny, inheritances, mandates, stars, godly scrolls, and every other implicated component of my life, arche, and metron.

9. I now receive a blood transfusion and new breath of life from Jesus Christ. In the process, I declare that all _____ circuitry, nanotech, back doors, front doors, side doors, trapdoors, inner doors, outer doors, ancient of days doors, infinite doors, hidden doors, cords, insects, vampiric structures, reset devices,

energy-draining devices, implants, wires, cables, chips, computers, chains, programs, backup programs, power sources, backup power sources, anomalous magnetic fields, gravitational manipulations, unified field, quantum regenerators, receptors, stardust, parallel timelines, counterfeit timelines, time warps, time dilation, time twisting, black holes, boxes, tesseracts, counterfeit galaxies, counterfeit constellations, counterfeit solar systems, counterfeit cosmoses, counterfeit universes, counterfeit heavens, counterfeit New Jerusalem, robots, embryos, parasites, pathogens, all artificial intelligences, all evil wave forms, fetuses, holograms, spiral staircases, amulets, clones, clocks, counterfeit temple elements (menorah, table of shew bread, ark of the covenant, mercy seat, bronze laver, altar of incense, molten sea, priestly garments, veils, Jachin and Boaz), data packets, ungodly grafts, and eggs are destroyed, and that all of their residue is purged with living water. I call back all of my DNA that was sold, traded, given away, or exchanged and housed in clones, machines, technologies, entities, banks, movies, and anything else illegitimately possessing it and call for it to be cleansed and healed with living water.

10. I now take authority over every evil spirit on the inside of me and around me that has been operating due to _____ and its interface points with my associated genetic

code, markers, cells of every type, meridian lines, chakras, energy signatures, acupuncture points, DNA strands, bone marrow, assignments, and blood. I declare that you are discovered, apprehended, bound, pierced through, and thrust out of me for judgment. I also discover every part that is a composite of genetic components of me and others associated with _____ and held together by a cord that binds. I declare that the cords are cut, that cords in cords are cut, and that all three-fold cords are cut, and that each part is separated into its components. All ungodly components, and components that are not of me, are now bound. I declare that all of them are now being sent to where the true Lord Jesus Christ sends them.

11. I pray that every spiritual object, tattoo, device, label, jewel, amulet, necklace, earring, rock, crown, sacred ring, wedding dress, looking glass, bracelet, charm, clock, garment, scepter, marker, power source, tracking device, system, grid, flower of life, branding, satanic scroll, Illuminati scroll, New World Order scroll, and all matrixes associated with any and all evil sacred orders placed in or around every part of me in order to anchor me to _____ would be consumed in the holy fire of Jesus Christ and totally dissolved, along with the infinite counterfeit crowns.

12. I call for every algorithm or formula created

from my DNA and genetic material that is projected throughout _____ to be shut down in every age, realm, dimension, frequency, vibration, and timeline, past, present, and future, to infinity, including all counterfeit and alternate creations. I command the immediate apprehension of all hybrids and every cosmic artificial intelligence and technology behind those projections and call for viruses encoded with heavenly algorithms to be uploaded into them and their computers in order to destroy them in judgment. I curse their computers with a curse of non-existence.

13. I identify every intergalactic and interplanetary data bank and computer that contains within its records or mainframe: data, equations, parts, algorithms, and information of any manner extracted from my humanity. I declare that angels are sent forth to liberate every part of me held captive in these data banks. I pray that all other records and information in them related to me would be forcefully erased and permanently deleted. I call for the lightning of God to destroy every ungodly altar (both sacrificial and honorary), as well as effigies contained within _____ representing me or bearing my name, image, or likeness, or in me, representing _____ and bearing its name, image, or likeness. I also call for the annulling and removal of every curse and ungodly insertion placed on the times and seasons of my

life in synchronicity with _____.
I receive synchronization with what has been written about me in the books of the Most High God.

14. Lastly, I surrender any and all counterfeit ephods (made up of a breastplate and power stones) to the True Lord Jesus Christ to be depowered and put in the place of his choosing. I pray that your lightning would now strike and sever any ungodly points of connectivity and demonic manipulation that remain between me and _____. I stand in my authority as a witness to cosmic injustice and as a child of the Most High God. I call for desynchronization between _____ and the genuine creation of God, galactic storms, and ley lines in the earth and throughout the cosmos. I call for desynchronization between _____ and earth's timelines, governments, nations, weather, financial systems, geosystems, human systems, and human domain. I call for an explosion of the light of Jesus Christ into the darkness of _____. I render this entire confession established in every timeline, age, realm, dimension, frequency, vibration, tree, planet, cosmos, constellation, and universe, past, present, and future, to infinity, and from the beginning across eternity. Amen.

FREEDOM FROM COMPUTERS
AND WALK-INS

This prayer is extensively detailed and oddly titled. The truth is that there may be times when a deliverance minister runs into something that seems to claim so many rights and legalities over a person that it considers the person's body to be their body. This level of bondage may be accompanied with a large amount of hardwiring, meaning the presence of actual implants under the skin that form a fully integrated interface with the entity in question. This prayer is titled as such because some of these entities are artificial intelligence-driven synthetic entities rooted in actual computers. Not all of these computers are built by humans, nor do they all exist on earth, so grounding out the need for this prayer with verifiable data is a challenge.

People are more familiar with the term "walk-in" because a trained trance medium may share his or her body and its function with another entity for extended periods of time. The language in this prayer has been tailored to secure a breakthrough under such circumstances. When it comes to the underlined space, you will put the name (or description) of the computer, synthetic entity, or walk-in that you have discovered. This can be discovered in a number of ways.

- If you are fortunate, the person knows the name of this entity in their presenting personality and can simply tell you.

- You can ask the Holy Spirit of Truth to reveal the name.

- If the person has connected with the True Lord Jesus Christ and can see him on the inside during healing and deliverance work, he will often provide this kind of information if asked. I will also instruct the person to look at Jesus on the inside first, and then I will ask the question.

- You can ask for the nearby angels to bind it on the right and on the left in golden bands and ask the angels to tell you its name.

- You can engage with the person's human spirit and ask for the name.

- You can engage with a soul-fragment living on the inside of the individual that claims to know the identity of the entity and is willing to talk.

- You can force the entity to the surface so that it is talking directly at you through the person's body and then try to get it to surrender its name (this is a last-case scenario in my approach).

Take note that in Point #3, there are four options. Depending on your current situation, you may find more peace with one option than another. Speak the option that provides you with the most peace. Do not speak all four.

1. Father in heaven, I come before you in the mighty name of Jesus Christ and I begin by anchoring this renunciation to _____ and all of his/her power sources, clones, holograms, twins, copies, facsimiles, duplicates, replicas, derivatives, replacements, or stand-ins, in every realm, age, timeline, dimension, frequency, vibration, planet, cosmos, constellation, and universe, past, present, and future, to infinity, and from the beginning across eternity, ensuring that no backup or reengagement or regeneration program or protocol will be able to engage upon his/her removal. I also deny access to any and all parts that the powers of darkness would take and traffic through doors in the floor, or other hidden doors to other planets or heavenly places during this renunciation as a back door to maintain hidden bondages in the name of Jesus.

2. I renounce my tethering to, overlaying and interfacing with, and all existence as _____ and all portals that are _____, including all related gates, paths, channels, and evil cosmic forces. I also

renounce all points of shared existence with my genetics, cells of every type, DNA strands, bone marrow, meridian lines, chakras, energy signatures, acupuncture points, anchors, and markers. I address all the powers of darkness associated with _____, including all related oversouls, parasites, implants, and quantum technologies, and serve them a bill of divorce. I pull up the hidden documents detailing every covenant, contract, agreement, certificate, oath, and vow entangling me and include all related books of wisdom, books of knowledge, books of philosophy, books of time travel, Freemasonic books, programming books, computational books, Keys of Solomon, genealogies of Cain, sacred texts of the Library of Alexandria and Vatican Library, and all other evil sacred books, and command that they be stamped with the blood of Jesus. I call for them to be nailed to the cross of Jesus Christ and burned with holy consuming fire.

3. In the name of Jesus, I pray that your heavenly hosts would be put on assignment to discover and apprehend every part, chakra, or gate belonging to me that is loyal to, affiliated with, or in bondage to _____.

   a. I pray that those parts would be escorted before the throne of the Father in heaven to be purged and completely healed and delivered.

   b. I pray that those parts would be escorted

to the feet of the Lion of the Tribe of Judah to be purged and completely healed and delivered.

    c. I pray that those parts would be put to sleep.

    d. I pray that those parts would be fired and sent to wherever the Lord Jesus sends them.

4. I now identify all territory and points of shared existence in me occupied by _____, including territory in my genetic code, markers, cells of every type, bone marrow, meridian lines, chakras, energy signatures, acupuncture points, DNA strands, and blood. I furthermore include all territory in my physical body (respiratory system, digestive system, cardiovascular system, renal system, endocrine system, nervous system, musculoskeletal system, exocrine system, glymphatic system, lymphatic system, immune system, sexual and reproductive system, and interstitia), all portions of my brain (prefrontal cortex, frontal lobe, temporal lobe, parietal lobe, occipital lobe, brain stem, corpus collosum, amygdala, hippocampus, HPA axis), and my entire internal Kabbalah tree (Keter, Binah, Chokhmah, Da'at, Gevurah, Hesed, Tif'eret, Hod, Netzach, Yesod, Malkhut, Occiput Interface, Counterfeit New Jerusalem) soul, spirit, implants, heart, decisions, worship, business, destiny, stars, offices, temple, subatomic particles, ministry, third eye, and

relationships. I deed the territory over to the kingdom of God and I invite you, Lord Jesus, to take the throne and to rule over this territory with your rod of iron.

5. In the name of Jesus, I now bind all gatekeepers and discover each and every portal access point associated with _____ and his/her interface points with my genetics, markers, cells of every type, meridian lines, chakras, energy signatures, acupuncture points, bone marrow, DNA strands, strongholds, internal Kabbalah tree, and blood, and all sentient intelligences, along with their agendas, connected realms, timelines, frequencies, vibrations, and all associated counterfeit inheritance.

6. I place the blood of Jesus upon every portal access point in all timelines, every realm, age, frequency, vibration, and dimension, past, present, and future, to infinity, and from the beginning across eternity, including all alternate and counterfeit creations, and I seal them with the Holy Spirit. I declare that they are put to sleep and permanently deactivated from this point in time and out of time, forward and backward and in every direction, inside out, upside down, back and forth, reversed, inverted, and vortexed.

7. I call for the identification of all reinforcement points, pillars, anchors, and structures. I pray that you would overtake these elements with your person, King Jesus. I appeal to my

heavenly mandate and call for the removal of every gate, frequency, barrier, equation, cloaking device, defensive protocol, force field, DNA matrix, apex of time, and sacred geometry that would otherwise block or guard these points and explode them all, along with all of their backups across time and space in Jesus's name. I also identify all cords and connective components binding artificial intelligence, reptilian genetics, octopus, star, machine and synthetic components, human parts, animal, insect or plant genetics and explode all of these connection points holding _____ together in Jesus's name.

8. I take the sword of the Spirit, which is the word of God, and I cut myself free from all ungodly tethers to, interfaces and overlays with, and all existence as _____ and all related satanic/Luciferian antiquities and iniquity. I also sever all paths, portals, frequencies, vibrations, gates, rivers, and light connecting _____ to any and all points in my internal Kabbalah tree and through it to the cosmic Kabbalistic tree of life and its related or derived realms. I call for the immediate apprehension and punishment of all entities traversing these paths, portals, frequencies, vibrations, gates, rivers, and light. I call the work sealed off and cauterized by the blood of Jesus. I liberate my genetics, markers, cells of every type, bone marrow, meridian lines, energy signatures, acupuncture points, DNA

strands, and blood. I deactivate my related chakra points. I sever all sentient intelligences, along with their agendas, related realms, timelines, and counterfeit inheritances, in Jesus's name.

9. I return every form of counterfeit inheritance associated with _____, inclusive of promised wealth, reward, position, status, calling, ability, power, roots, pride, genetic code, anything lying dormant, ungodly structures, ungodly grafts, counterfeit citizenship, ungodly citizenship, super-soldier status, and all associated rites of passage, and any other form of counterfeit inheritance, in Jesus's name. I refuse it and sever myself from it, including all forms of worship and deification of _____, and from this point in time and out of time, forward and backward and in every direction, inside out, upside down, back and forth, reversed, inverted, and vortexed, I choose to receive my inheritance in Jesus Christ. I also declare your Word in Proverbs 13:22, which says that the wealth of the wicked is stored up for the just. I receive the wealth, freedom, giftings, and abilities held hostage by _____ as a recipient of wealth transfer in Jesus's name. Furthermore, my physical children, and children's children, are an inheritance in Jesus Christ, and I receive them and their redemption in Jesus Christ, and renounce all of their debts to _____. I renounce

all spirit children and ungodly offspring related to _____ and undo all quantum entanglements involved in their creation. I command their judgment and the purging of the spaces and realms they occupy (or interface with) by judgment through living water mingled with all-consuming fire.

10. I renounce all ungodly paternal and maternal claims, sponsorships and affiliations, apprenticeships, royal appointments, marriage ceremonies, offices and council appointments, and oneness with all persons and entities associated with _____. I pray for an annulling of all associated dedications, ceremonies, scientific processes, and celebrations. In doing so, I now declare reversal upon every ungodly pronouncement and judgment passed against my spirit, soul, and body, my household, offspring, finances, marriage, destiny, inheritances, mandates, stars, godly scrolls, and every other implicated component of my life, arche, and metron.

11. I now receive a blood transfusion and new breath of life from Jesus Christ. In the process, I declare that all _____ circuitry, nanotech, back doors, front doors, side doors, trapdoors, inner doors, outer doors, ancient of days doors, infinite doors, hidden doors, cords, insects, vampiric structures, reset devices, energy-draining devices, implants, wires, cables, chips, computers, chains,

programs, backup programs, power sources, backup power sources, anomalous magnetic fields, gravitational manipulations, unified field, quantum regenerators, receptors, stardust, parallel timelines, counterfeit timelines, time warps, time dilation, black holes, boxes, tesseracts, counterfeit galaxies, counterfeit constellations, counterfeit solar systems, counterfeit cosmoses, counterfeit universes, counterfeit heavens, counterfeit New Jerusalem, robots, embryos, parasites, pathogens, trading floors, bioweapons, all artificial intelligences, all evil wave forms, fetuses, holograms, spiral staircases, amulets, clones, clocks, counterfeit temple elements, data packets, ungodly grafts, and eggs are destroyed, and that all of their residue is purged with living water. I call back all of my DNA that was sold, buried, traded, given away, or exchanged and housed in clones, machines, technologies, entities, banks, movies, or in containers in deep recesses of my person, and anything else illegitimately possessing it, and call for it to be cleansed and healed with living water.

12. I now take authority over every evil spirit on the inside of me and around me that has been operating due to _____ and his/her interface points with my associated genetic code, markers, cells of every type, meridian lines, chakras, energy signatures, acupuncture points, DNA strands, bone

marrow, assignments, and blood. I declare that you are discovered, apprehended, bound, pierced through, and thrust out of me for judgment. I also discover every part that is a composite of genetic components of me and _____ held together by a cord that binds, and all other manifestations of oneness. I declare that the cords are cut, that cords in cords are cut, and that all three-fold cords are cut, and that each part is separated into its components. All ungodly components, and components that are not of me, are now bound. I declare that all of them are now being sent to where the true Lord Jesus Christ sends them.

13. I pray that every spiritual object, tattoo, device, label, jewel, amulet, necklace, earring, rock, crown, sacred ring, wedding dress, wedding veil, keyboard, looking glass, bracelet, charm, clock, garment, scepter, marker, power source, tracking device, system, grid, flower of life, branding, satanic scroll, Illuminati scroll, New World Order scroll, super-soldier scroll, and all matrixes associated with any and all evil sacred orders placed in or around every part of me in order to anchor me to _____ and reinforce our shared existence would be consumed in the holy fire of Jesus Christ and totally dissolved.

14. I call for every algorithm or formula created from my DNA and genetic material that is

projected throughout _____ to be shut down in every age, realm, dimension, frequency, vibration, and timeline, past, present and future, to infinity, including all counterfeit and alternate creations. I command the immediate apprehension of all hybrids and every cosmic artificial intelligence and technology behind those projections and call for viruses encoded with heavenly algorithms to be uploaded into them and their computers in order to destroy them in judgment. I curse their computers with a curse of non-existence. I petition you, King Jesus, to inject your formula that undoes the imprint of the DNA. I pray that you would override all password-protected regions that are guarded by ungodly formulas with your keys and expose all of the enemy's strongholds and take them out with your armies.

15. I identify every intergalactic and interplanetary data bank and computer that contains within its records or mainframe: data, equations, parts, algorithms, and information of any manner extracted from my humanity. I declare that angels are sent forth to liberate every part of me held captive in these data banks. I pray that all other records and information in them related to me would be forcefully erased and permanently deleted. I call for the lightning of God to destroy every ungodly altar (both sacrificial and honorary) as well as effigies contained within _____

representing me or bearing my name, image, or likeness, or in me, representing _____ and bearing his/her name, image, or likeness. I also call for the annulling and removal of every curse and ungodly insertion placed on the times and seasons of my life in synchronicity with _____. I receive synchronization with what has been written about me in the books of the Most High God.

16. Lastly, I pray that your lightning would now strike and sever any ungodly points of connectivity and demonic manipulation that remain between me and _____. I stand in my authority as a witness to cosmic injustice and as a child of the Most High God. I call for desynchronization between _____ and me, authored by the voice of the Most High God. I also call for _____ to reap a hundredfold return for the evil that has been sown against me in the form of judgment and wrath, the razor of the Lord, the broom of destruction, and the whirlwind of God, tsunamis of living water, and ravenous birds that will devour his/her flesh. I render this entire confession established in every timeline, age, realm, dimension, tree, frequency, vibration, planet, cosmos, constellation, and universe, past, present, and future, to infinity, and from the beginning across eternity. Amen.

FREEDOM FROM
SYNTHETIC KINGDOMS

This prayer is similar to some of my other prayers except that it is specific to the synthetic kingdoms. This is hopefully a one and done, but if people are aggressively tethered into the synthetic kingdoms, their freedom will likely come in layers. Therefore, one may find themselves saying this renunciation over and over during a season of deliverance.

As to instructions on how to use this prayer, they are simple. Say it. There is nothing to discern and nothing to plug into a blank space. If you have crazy, off-the-charts deliverance, praise God! If not much happens, then this isn't likely to be your problem. In the book *Prayers that Shake Heaven and Earth*, I included a prayer for freedom from Synthetic Genetics. This prayer is like that prayer on steroids. This is going to be especially applicable to those that have experienced many abductions, come from military families, or experienced strange interactions and interfaces with technologies like computers and cell phones.

Take note that in Point #3 of the prayer, there are four options. Depending on your current situation, you may find more peace with one option than another. Speak the option that provides you with the most peace. Do not speak all four.

1. Father in heaven, I come before you in the mighty name of Jesus Christ and I begin by anchoring this renunciation to the electrical, magnetic, robotic, artificial intelligence, holographic, and synthetic kingdoms, and all related power sources, clones, holograms, twins, copies, facsimiles, duplicates, replicas, derivatives, replacements, or stand-ins, in every realm, age, timeline, dimension, frequency, vibration, planet, cosmos, constellation, and universe, past, present, and future, to infinity, and from the beginning across eternity, ensuring that no backup, reengagement, or regeneration program or protocol will be able to engage upon untethering. I also deny access to any and all parts that the powers of darkness would take and traffic through doors in the floor, or other hidden doors to other planets or heavenly places during this renunciation as a back door to maintain hidden bondages in the name of Jesus.

2. I renounce my tethering to, overlaying and interfacing with, and all existence as the electrical, magnetic, robotic, artificial intelligence, holographic, and synthetic kingdoms, and all portals that are these kingdoms, including all related gates, paths, channels, and evil cosmic forces. I also

renounce all points of shared existence with my genetics, cells of every type, DNA strands, bone marrow, meridian lines, chakras, energy signatures, acupuncture points, anchors, and markers. I address all the powers of darkness associated with these kingdoms, including all related oversouls, parasites, implants, and quantum technologies, and serve them a bill of divorce. I pull up the hidden documents detailing every covenant, contract, agreement, certificate, oath, and vow entangling me and include all related books of wisdom, books of knowledge, books of philosophy, books of time travel, Freemasonic books, programming books, computational books, Keys of Solomon, genealogies of Cain, sacred texts of the Library of Alexandria and Vatican Library, and all other evil sacred books, and command that they be stamped with the blood of Jesus. I call for them to be nailed to the cross of Jesus Christ and burned with holy consuming fire.

3. In the name of Jesus, I pray that your heavenly hosts would be put on assignment to discover and apprehend every part, chakra, or gate belonging to me that is loyal to, affiliated with, or in bondage to the electrical, magnetic, robotic, artificial intelligence, holographic, and synthetic kingdoms.

   a. I pray that those parts would be escorted before the throne of the Father in heaven to be purged of their related components and completely healed and delivered.

b. I pray that those parts would be escorted to the feet of the Lion of the Tribe of Judah to be purged of their related components and completely healed and delivered.

c. I pray that those parts would be put to sleep.

d. I pray that those parts would be fired and sent to wherever the Lord Jesus sends them.

4. I now identify all territory and points of shared existence in me occupied by the electrical, magnetic, robotic, artificial intelligence, holographic, and synthetic kingdoms, including territory in my genetic code, markers, cells of every type, bone marrow, meridian lines, chakras, energy signatures, acupuncture points, DNA strands, and blood. I furthermore include all territory in my physical body (respiratory system, digestive system, cardiovascular system, renal system, endocrine system, nervous system, musculoskeletal system, exocrine system, glymphatic system, lymphatic system, immune system, sexual and reproductive system, and interstitia), all portions of my brain (prefrontal cortex, frontal lobe, temporal lobe, parietal lobe, occipital lobe, brain stem, corpus collosum, amygdala, hippocampus, HPA axis), and my entire internal Kabbalah tree (Keter, Binah, Chokhmah,

Da'at, Gevurah, Hesed, Tif'eret, Hod, Netzach, Yesod, Malkhut, Occiput Interface, Counterfeit New Jerusalem), soul, spirit, implants, heart, decisions, worship, business, destiny, stars, offices, temple, subatomic particles, ministry, third eye, and relationships. I deed the territory over to the kingdom of God and I invite you, Lord Jesus, to take the throne and to rule over this territory with your rod of iron.

5. In the name of Jesus, I now bind all gatekeepers and discover each and every portal access point associated with the electrical, magnetic, robotic, artificial intelligence, holographic, and synthetic kingdoms and their interface points with my genetics, markers, cells of every type, meridian lines, chakras, energy signatures, acupuncture points, bone marrow, DNA strands, strongholds, internal Kabbalah tree, blood, and all sentient intelligences, along with their agendas, connected realms, timelines, frequencies, vibrations, and all associated counterfeit inheritance.

6. I place the blood of Jesus upon every portal access point in all timelines, every realm, age, frequency, vibration, and dimension, past, present, and future, to infinity, and from the beginning across eternity, including all alternate and counterfeit creations, and I seal them with the Holy Spirit. I declare that they are put to sleep and permanently deactivated from this point in time and out of time, forward

and backward and in every direction, inside out, upside down, back and forth, reversed, inverted, and vortexed.

7. I call for the identification of all reinforcement points, pillars, anchors, and structures. I pray that you would overtake these elements with your person, King Jesus. I appeal to my heavenly mandate and call for the removal of every gate, frequency, barrier, equation, cloaking device, defensive protocol, force field, DNA matrix, apex of time, and sacred geometry that would otherwise block or guard these points and explode them all, along with all of their backups across time and space in Jesus's name. I also identify all cords and connective components binding artificial intelligence, machine and synthetic components, human parts, foreign genetics, quantum computers, holographic computers, and devices of demonic or cosmic origins and explode all of these elements along with all connection points binding me to the electrical, magnetic, robotic, artificial intelligence, holographic, and synthetic kingdoms in Jesus's name.

8. I take the sword of the Spirit, which is the word of God, and I cut myself free from all ungodly tethers to, interfaces and overlays with, and all existence as the electrical, magnetic, robotic, artificial intelligence, holographic, and synthetic kingdoms and all related satanic/ Luciferian antiquities and iniquity. I also sever

all paths, portals, frequencies, vibrations, gates, rivers, and light connecting these kingdoms to any and all points in my internal Kabbalah tree and through it to the cosmic Kabbalistic tree of life and its related or derived realms. I call for the immediate apprehension and punishment of all entities traversing these paths, portals, frequencies, vibrations, gates, rivers, and light. I call the work sealed off and cauterized by the blood of Jesus. I liberate my genetics, markers, cells of every type, bone marrow, meridian lines, energy signatures, acupuncture points, DNA strands, and blood. I deactivate my related chakra points. I sever all sentient intelligences, along with their agendas, related realms, timelines, and counterfeit inheritances, in Jesus's name.

9. I return every form of counterfeit inheritance associated with the electrical, magnetic, robotic, artificial intelligence, holographic, and synthetic kingdoms, inclusive of promised wealth, reward, position, status, calling, ability, power, roots, pride, genetic code, anything lying dormant, ungodly structures, ungodly grafts, counterfeit citizenship, ungodly citizenship, super-soldier status, and all associated rites of passage, and any other form of counterfeit inheritance, in Jesus's name. I refuse it and sever myself from it, including all forms of worship and deification of these kingdoms or their rulers, and from this point in time and out of time, forward and backward and in

every direction, inside out, upside down, back and forth, reversed, inverted, and vortexed, I choose to receive my inheritance in Jesus Christ. I also declare your Word in Proverbs 13:22, which says that the wealth of the wicked is stored up for the just. I receive the wealth, freedom, giftings, and abilities held hostage by these kingdoms as a recipient of wealth transfer in Jesus's name. Furthermore, my physical children, and children's children, are an inheritance in Jesus Christ, and I receive them and their redemption in Jesus Christ and renounce all of their debts to these kingdoms. I renounce all spirit children and ungodly offspring related to these kingdoms and undo all quantum entanglements involved in their creation. I command their judgment and the purging of the spaces and realms they occupy (or interfaced with) by judgment through living water mingled with all-consuming fire.

10. I renounce all ungodly paternal and maternal claims, sponsorships and affiliations, apprenticeships, royal appointments, marriage ceremonies, offices and council appointments, and oneness with all persons and entities associated with the electrical, magnetic, robotic, artificial intelligence, holographic, and synthetic kingdoms. I pray for an annulling of all associated dedications, ceremonies, scientific processes, and celebrations. In doing so, I now declare reversal upon every ungodly pronouncement and judgment passed against

my spirit, soul, and body, my household, offspring, finances, marriage, destiny, inheritances, mandates, stars, godly scrolls, and every other implicated component of my life, arche, and metron.

11. I now receive a blood transfusion and new breath of life from Jesus Christ. In the process, I declare that all of the electrical, magnetic, robotic, artificial intelligence, holographic, and synthetic kingdom circuitry, nanotech, back doors, front doors, side doors, trapdoors, inner doors, outer doors, ancient of days doors, infinite doors, hidden doors, cords, insects, vampiric structures, reset devices, energy-draining devices, implants, wires, cables, chips, computers, chains, programs, backup programs, power sources, backup power sources, anomalous magnetic fields, gravitational manipulations, unified field, quantum regenerators, receptors, stardust, parallel timelines, counterfeit timelines, time warps, time dilation, black holes, boxes, tesseracts, counterfeit galaxies, counterfeit constellations, counterfeit solar systems, counterfeit cosmoses, counterfeit universes, counterfeit heavens, counterfeit New Jerusalem, robots, embryos, parasites, pathogens, trading floors, bioweapons, all artificial intelligences, all evil wave forms, fetuses, holograms, spiral staircases, amulets, clones, clocks, counterfeit temple elements, data packets, ungodly grafts, and eggs are

destroyed, and that all of their residue is purged with living water. I call back all of my DNA that was sold, buried, traded, given away, or exchanged and housed in clones, machines, technologies, entities, banks, movies, or in containers in deep recesses of my person, and anything else illegitimately possessing it, and call for it to be cleansed and healed with living water.

12. I now take authority over every evil spirit on the inside of me and around me that has been operating due to the electrical, magnetic, robotic, artificial intelligence, holographic, and synthetic kingdoms and their interface points with my associated genetic code, markers, cells of every type, meridian lines, chakras, energy signatures, acupuncture points, DNA strands, bone marrow, assignments, and blood. I declare that you are discovered, apprehended, bound, pierced through, and thrust out of me for judgment. I also discover every part that is a composite of genetic components of me and others in these kingdoms held together by a cord that binds, and all other manifestations of oneness. I declare that the cords are cut, that cords in cords are cut, and that all three-fold cords are cut, and that each part is separated into its components. All ungodly components, and components that are not of me, are now bound. I declare that all of them are now being sent to where the true Lord Jesus Christ sends them.

13. I pray that every spiritual object, tattoo, device, label, jewel, amulet, necklace, earring, rock, crown, sacred ring, wedding dress, wedding veil, looking glass, bracelet, charm, clock, garment, scepter, marker, power source, tracking device, system, grid, flower of life, branding, satanic scroll, Illuminati scroll, New World Order scroll, super-soldier scroll, and all matrixes associated with any and all evil sacred orders placed in or around every part of me in order to anchor me to the electrical, magnetic, robotic, artificial intelligence, holographic, and synthetic kingdoms and reinforce our shared existence would be consumed in the holy fire of Jesus Christ and totally dissolved.

14. I call for every algorithm or formula created from my DNA and genetic material that is projected throughout the electrical, magnetic, robotic, artificial intelligence, holographic, and synthetic kingdoms to be shut down in every age, realm, dimension, frequency, vibration, and timeline, past, present, and future, to infinity, including all counterfeit and alternate creations. I command the immediate apprehension of all hybrids, robots, and every cosmic artificial intelligence and technology behind those projections and call for viruses encoded with heavenly algorithms to be uploaded into them and their computers in order to destroy them in judgment. I curse their computers with a curse of non-existence. I petition you, King Jesus, to inject your

formula that undoes the imprint of the DNA. I pray that you would override all password-protected regions that are guarded by ungodly formulas with your keys and expose all of the enemy's strongholds and take them out with your armies.

15. I identify every intergalactic and interplanetary data bank and computer that contains within its records or mainframe: data, equations, parts, algorithms, and information of any manner extracted from my humanity. I declare that angels are sent forth to liberate every part of me held captive in these data banks. I pray that all other records and information in them related to me would be forcefully erased and permanently deleted. I call for the lightning of God to destroy every ungodly altar (both sacrificial and honorary), as well as effigies contained within the electrical, magnetic, robotic, artificial intelligence, holographic, and synthetic kingdoms representing me or bearing my name, image, or likeness, or in me, representing these kingdoms and bearing their names, images, or likenesses. I also call for the annulling and removal of every curse and ungodly insertion placed on the times and seasons of my life in synchronicity with these kingdoms. I receive synchronization with what has been written about me in the books of the Most High God.

16. Lastly, I pray that your lightning would

now strike and sever any ungodly points of connectivity and demonic manipulation that remain between me and the electrical, magnetic, robotic, artificial intelligence, holographic, and synthetic kingdoms. I stand in my authority as a witness to cosmic injustice and as a child of the Most High God. I call for desynchronization between these kingdoms and me authored by the voice of the Most High God. I also call for evil components of these kingdoms to reap a hundredfold return for the evil that has been sown against me in the form of judgment and wrath, the razor of the Lord, the broom of the Lord, and the whirlwind of God, tsunamis of living water, and the hot thunderbolt of God. I render this entire confession established in every timeline, age, realm, dimension, frequency, vibration, planet, cosmos, constellation, and universe, past, present, and future, to infinity, and from the beginning across eternity. Amen.

PRAYER OF RELEASE

In the book *Prayers that Shake Heaven and Earth,* I included two prayers that were exceptionally good at separating people from their human persecutors in both the natural and the spirit. These prayers helped thousands that were being pursued by witches, warlocks, ex-lovers, bullies, evil bosses, and a host of other individuals. This prayer was called the Freedom from Human Persecutors Prayer, and the second version was called Freedom from Human Persecutors 2.0. The problem that several people ran into, however, is that the language wasn't ideal when they were married in the natural to the person that was persecuting them in the spirit. Also, many people found the language of that prayer particularly difficult to apply to parents or children, even though aspects of the prayers were necessary to put healthy spiritual boundaries back in place.

This prayer can be used by those who have lost loved ones to death and haven't fully transitioned out of grief, becoming able to release their loved ones from their hearts. This prayer can also be used by children of parents where codependent relationships are in place, or vice versa. The language of this prayer is ideal for spouses that are in unhealthy marriages that contain physical, sexual, psychological, or verbal mistreatment. If you are waking up to the reality that you have satanic ritual abuse in your background, you will want to use this prayer for your children, because even if you haven't knowingly done anything evil to your children, it is quite possible that you have cult-loyal soul parts that have, even if only from the spirit realm.

There is another category as well. Some people that are coming to Christ are abusers. Yes, you imprisoned people's souls, you spoke curses, and you subdued the destiny of others. You derailed the lives of your own children through your physical, sexual, and verbal misconduct. It is often much easier for people to relate to the ways in which they were victimized than to own up to the ways that they abused, hurt, and derailed others, especially if the things that were done are crimes that could be sentenced in a court of law. Nonetheless, when a person that has been an abuser comes to a place of repentance, they need to release the people they have enslaved, hurt, and in some cases, destroyed. This prayer will help the repentant abuser do just that.

Take note that in Point #2 of the prayer, there are four options. Depending on your current situation, you may find more peace with one option than another. Speak the option that provides you with the most peace. Do not speak all four.

1. Father in heaven, I come before you in the mighty name of Jesus Christ and I release _____. I pull up the hidden documents detailing every unholy covenant, contract, agreement, certificate, oath, and vow entangling us and include all related books of wisdom, books of knowledge, books of philosophy, books of time travel, Freemasonic books, programming books, computational books, and all other evil sacred books, and command that they be stamped with the blood of Jesus. I call for them to be nailed to the cross of Jesus Christ and burned with holy consuming fire.

2. In the name of Jesus, I pray that your heavenly hosts would place every part belonging to me that is against this act on temporary lockdown.

   a. I pray that those parts would be escorted before the throne of the Father in heaven to receive ministry.

   b. I pray that those parts would be escorted to the feet of the Lion of the Tribe of Judah to receive ministry.

   c. I pray that those parts would be put to sleep.

   d. I pray that those parts would be fired and sent to wherever the Lord Jesus sends them.

3. I now deed all territory where _____ is held captive in me, around me, or in any way entangled with or connected to me, over to the kingdom of God and I invite you, Lord Jesus, to take the throne and to rule over this territory with your rod of iron. I call for the liberation of every prison, dungeon, castle, hospital, laboratory, or facility binding any part of his/her person, including his/her soul, spirit, heart, decisions, worship, business, ministry, destiny, stars, offices, temple, subatomic particles, and relationships.

4. In the name of Jesus, I now bind all gatekeepers, and discover each and every portal access point connecting us and allowing for unholy traffic between us.

5. I place the blood of Jesus upon every portal access point and I seal them with the Holy Spirit. I declare that they are put to sleep and permanently deactivated from this point in time and out of time, forward and backward and in every direction.

6. I take the sword of the Spirit, which is the word of God, and I sever _____ from myself in every ungodly way that he/she has been entangled. I call for angels to untangle and separate us, escorting our parts to the places where they belong.

7. I speak that every form of our respective

spiritual inheritances is untangled and separated out, inclusive of promised wealth, position, status, calling, ability, power, roots, favors, seed, and any other form of inheritance, in Jesus's name. From this point in time and out of time, forward and backward and in every direction, I choose to receive my inheritance in Jesus Christ. I renounce all spirit children related to _____ and undo all quantum entanglements involved in their creation. I command their judgment and the purging of the realms they occupy by judgment through living water. I also reclaim and receive every part of me that has been imprisoned by _____ or in realms related to him/her.

8. I release forgiveness by faith to _____ for the evil that he/she has done against me. I also choose to forgive myself for all of the evil that I have performed against _____. I also discover every part that is a composite of our genetic components that are held together by a cord that binds. I declare that the cords are cut and that each part is separated into its components. I retain my parts and surrender those that do not belong to me. I command your heavenly hosts to bind every part of _____ in me and take him/her where he/she belongs now. All hiding places are exposed right now. I

declare that he/she cannot hide or escape.

9. I now take authority over every evil spirit on the inside of _____ and around him/her that has been operating under my authority or the authority of my parts. I annul every curse, verdict, and evil judgment I have rendered against him/her by the power of the blood of Jesus and declare that every evil spirit is now sent to wherever the Lord Jesus sends them. I also declare that every evil spirit on the inside of me and around me that has been operating under the authority of _____ is discovered, apprehended, bound, pierced through, and thrust out of me for judgment. I declare that they are sent to wherever the Lord Jesus sends them right now.

10. Lastly, I pray that every spiritual object, tattoo, device, label, jewel, amulet, necklace, earring, crown, ring, garment, scepter, marker, power source, tracking device, system, grid, or branding placed in or around every part of _____ by me or any part of me or those under my authority, or in me placed by _____ or any part of him/her or those under his/her authority, would be consumed in the holy fire of Jesus Christ and totally dissolved. I render this entire confession established in every timeline, age, realm, dimension, frequency, vibration, planet, cosmos, constellation, and universe,

past, present, and future, to infinity, and from the beginning across eternity. Amen.

ULTIMATE FREEDOM
FROM HUMAN
PERSECUTORS PRAYER

Dealing with high-level witches and warlocks that are heavily vested in your manipulation, control, and destruction can be extraordinarily difficult to overcome. In the book *Prayers that Shake Heaven and Earth*, two prayers were provided for breaking free from human persecutors. Despite the incredible amount of legalities that were covered in the Freedom from Human Persecutors 2.0 prayer, I found that it still wasn't enough to get the job done in some cases. Thus, I have compiled this prayer with input from others that needed it for their situations. It is by far the longest and most grueling prayer you will find in my collection of deliverance prayers as of the publication of this work. It is a mega prayer that I hope most folks will not have to resort to. If you do find this prayer necessary, just be sure to set aside some time, because this will not be a 10-minute experience. Into the blank space, you will put the name or description of the person that you need to be separated from.

1. Father in heaven, I come boldly before your throne of grace to find mercy and grace to help in time of need. I enter into your gates with

thanksgiving and I enter into your courts with praise. I hide myself in Christ Jesus, and from this secret place, I perform this renunciation and divorce. I command that every gate, frequency, barrier, equation, cloaking device, force field, sacred geometry, DNA matrix, apex of time, formula, defensive protocol, and any other form of unholy technology that would otherwise hinder progress, conceal ungodly agents, agendas, and/or activities in relation to this renunciation and divorce of _____ would be deactivated, disengaged, and moved out of the way, including all connected bombs, trip wires, and booby traps.

2. I speak that this renunciation and divorce is executed against a conglomerate, which includes _____ along with every unholy title and every being that has ever or will ever be part of and/or connected with _____ in any unholy way, including but not limited to his/her family lines as revealed in the heavenly cosmic records, all related bloodlines, stolen lines, unholy engrafted lines, unholy trading lines, unholy soul lines, unholy body lines, unholy synthetic lines, evil entity lines, and all other connected unholy lines in every realm, age, timeline, dimension, frequency, vibration, planet, cosmos, constellation, and universe, past, present, and future, to infinity, and from the beginning across eternity. I declare that

this conglomerate will henceforth be referred to as the group.

3. I renounce my tethering to, overlaying and interfacing with, and all existence as the group and all portals that are the group and all associated gates, paths, channels, forces, genetic and cellular anchoring, data packets, ungodly DNA strands, bone marrow, assignments, blood, markers, meridian lines, chakras, energy signatures, neural lace, all related powers of darkness, quantum technologies, oversouls, and any other type of malevolent being in every realm, age, timeline, dimension, frequency, vibration, planet, cosmos, constellation, and universe, past, present, and future, to infinity, and from the beginning across eternity, and serve them a bill of divorce. I pull up the hidden documents and code detailing every covenant, unholy ritualistic act, enslavement, agreement, contract, certificate, oath, and vow entangling me, my God-assigned family line, and my God-assigned bloodline, and command that they be stamped with the blood of Jesus.

4. I pray that your heavenly hosts would discover, apprehend, and deliver every part, chakra, or gate belonging to me that is loyal to, affiliated with, or in bondage to the group and escort them to the feet of the Lion of the Tribe of Judah. I declare that every part or region in me that is bound to the group, and/or any entity

under the authority of the group by a cord that binds, must now be cut free and delivered. I speak that the cords are cut, that cords in cords are cut, and that all three-fold cords are cut, and that each part or region is separated into its components. All ungodly components and components that are not of me are now bound. I declare that all of them are now being sent to where the true Lord Jesus Christ sends them.

5. I command that every binding mechanism and/or subdue mechanism must be removed. I decree that all chains, shackles, dirty garments, and other forms of bondage are removed. I decree that all evil projections of fear, shame, guilt, rejection, and/or any related form of darkness must be removed, along with all ungodly canopies and essences. Lord Jesus, I pray for a release of your blood inside and outside of these areas, fully infusing these areas. I pray for a release of your healing balm of Gilead into all of these areas. I declare your peace over all of these areas.

6. I now deed all territory in me, my sphere, realm, residence, God-given timeline, and everywhere assigned to me by God, past, present, and future, to infinity, that is occupied by the group and all associated genetic and/ or cellular anchoring, data packets, markers, bone marrow, assignments, ungodly DNA strands, neural lace, chakras, meridian lines, energy signatures, and blood, and all sentient

intelligences along with their agendas, connected realms, computers, domains, and timelines, over to the kingdom of God. I furthermore include all territory in my physical body (respiratory system, digestive system, cardiovascular system, renal system, endocrine system, nervous system, musculoskeletal system, exocrine system, glymphatic system, lymphatic system, immune system, sexual and reproductive system, and interstitia), all portions of my brain (prefrontal cortex, frontal lobe, temporal lobe, parietal lobe, occipital lobe, brain stem, corpus collosum, amygdala, hippocampus, HPA axis), and my entire internal Kabbalah tree (Keter, Binah, Chokhmah, Da'at, Gevurah, Hesed, Tif'eret, Hod, Netzach, Yesod, Malkhut, Occiput Interface, Counterfeit New Jerusalem), soul, spirit, implants, heart, decisions, worship, business, destiny, stars, offices, temple, subatomic particles, ministry, and relationships and I invite you, Lord Jesus, to take the throne and to rule over this territory with your rod of iron.

7. In the name of Jesus, I now bind all gatekeepers and discover each and every portal access point associated with the group and all associated genetic and/or cellular anchoring, data packets, markers, bone marrow, neural lace, ungodly DNA strands, blood, and all sentient intelligences along with their agendas, connected realms, computers, domains, timelines, and all associated counterfeit

inheritance.

8. I place the blood of Jesus inside and outside of every portal access point in every realm, age, timeline, dimension, frequency, vibration, planet, cosmos, constellation, and universe, past, present, and future, to infinity, and from the beginning across eternity, and I collapse, close, and seal them by the power of the blood of Jesus and the Holy Spirit. I declare that they are put to sleep and permanently deactivated from this point in time and out of time, forward and backward and in every direction, inside out, upside down, back and forth, reversed, inverted, and vortexed.

9. I take the sword of the spirit, which is the word of God, and I cut myself free from all ungodly tethers to, interfaces and overlays with, and all existence of the group and all related satanic/ Luciferian antiquities and iniquity. I also sever all paths, portals, frequencies, vibrations, gates, rivers, and light connecting the group to any and all points in my internal Kabbalah tree and through it to the cosmic Kabbalistic tree of life and its related or derived realms. I call for the immediate apprehension and punishment of all entities traversing these paths, portals, frequencies, vibrations, gates, rivers, and light. I call the work sealed off and cauterized by the blood of Jesus. I liberate my genetics, markers, cells of every type, bone marrow, meridian lines, energy signatures,

acupuncture points, DNA strands, and blood. I deactivate my related chakra points. I sever all sentient intelligences, along with their agendas, related realms, timelines, and counterfeit inheritances, in Jesus's name. I furthermore sever myself (body, spirit, soul, and heart) from all attachment points and points of connectivity belonging to the group on my reproductive organs (vagina, ovaries, cervix, pelvic floor, breasts, fallopian tubes, uterus, womb and eggs/penis, testicles, sperm) hips, back, adrenal glands, pineal gland, and every other organ, body part, or area of my body, soul, or spirit in bondage in every realm, age, timeline, and dimension, past, present, and future, to infinity. I pray that the connection points would be cauterized and sealed with the Holy Spirit.

10. I return every form of counterfeit inheritance, inclusive of promised wealth, position, status, calling, ability, power, pride, genetic code, seed, jewel, necklace, earring, crown, ring, scepter, wedding ring, garment, and any other form of counterfeit inheritance from the group. I refuse it and sever myself from it, and from this point in time and out of time, forward and backward and in every direction, inside out, upside down, back and forth, reversed, inverted, and vortexed, I choose to receive my inheritance in Jesus Christ. I also declare your Word in Proverbs 13:22, which says that the wealth of the wicked is stored up for the just. I

receive the wealth held hostage by the group and their kingdoms as a recipient of wealth transfer in Jesus's name. Furthermore, my physical children, and children's children, are an inheritance in Jesus Christ, and I renounce all of their debts to the group. I renounce and sever myself from all ungodly offspring and spirit children related to the group and their kingdoms and undo all quantum entanglements involved in their creation. I command their judgment and the purging of the realms they occupy by judgment through living water mingled with all-consuming fire.

11. I now receive a blood transfusion and new breath of life from Jesus Christ. In the process, I declare that all of the group's circuitry, nanotech, back doors, front doors, side doors, trapdoors, inner doors, outer doors, ancient of days doors, infinite doors, hidden doors, cords, insects, vampiric structures, reset devices, energy-draining devices, implants, wires, cables, chips, computers, chains, programs, backup programs, power sources, backup power sources, anomalous magnetic fields, gravitational manipulations, unified field, quantum regenerators, receptors, stardust, parallel timelines, counterfeit timelines, time warps, time dilation, black holes, boxes, tesseracts, counterfeit galaxies, counterfeit constellations, counterfeit solar systems, counterfeit cosmoses, counterfeit universes, counterfeit heavens, counterfeit

New Jerusalem, robots, embryos, parasites, pathogens, all artificial intelligences, all evil wave forms, fetuses, holograms, spiral staircases, amulets, clones, clocks, counterfeit temple elements (menorah, table of shew bread, ark of the covenant, mercy seat, bronze laver, altar of incense, molten sea, priestly garments, veils, Jachin and Boaz), data packets, ungodly grafts, and eggs are destroyed, and that all of their residue is purged with living water. I declare to the impacted cells, receive healing and recalibration from Jesus Christ. Lord Jesus, I apply your living water along the pathways created and carved for access. I call back all of my DNA that was sold, buried, traded, given away, or exchanged and housed in clones, animals, machines, technologies, entities, banks, movies, or in containers in deep recesses of my person, and anything else illegitimately possessing it, and call for it to be cleansed and healed with living water.

12. I release forgiveness by faith to the group for the injustice they have executed against me and my household. I now take authority over every human, hybrid, synthetic entity, zombie, evil entity, malevolent being, and being not assigned by God on the inside of me and/or around me, my realm, and my sphere of influence that has been operating due to the group and all related genetic and cellular anchoring, markers, ungodly DNA strands, neural lace, bone marrow, meridian

lines, chakras, energy signatures, assignments, and blood. I declare that you are discovered, apprehended, bound, pierced through, and thrust out of me for judgment. I specifically address disembodied ancestral spirits and every other being not assigned by God on the inside of me and/or around me that is loyal to the group. I decree that your documents and rights, inclusive of all covenants with death, are annulled by the blood of Jesus. I decree that you are evicted now. All evil entity components, demonic components, human components, synthetic components, and components that are not of me are now bound and sent to where the true Lord Jesus Christ sends them.

13. I renounce all ungodly paternal and maternal claims, sponsorships and affiliations, apprenticeships, royal appointments, marriage ceremonies, offices and council appointments, and oneness with all persons and entities associated with the group. I pray for an annulling of all associated dedications, ceremonies, scientific processes, and celebrations. In doing so, I now declare reversal upon every ungodly pronouncement and judgment passed against my spirit, soul, and body, my household, offspring, finances, marriage, destiny, inheritances, mandates, stars, godly scrolls, and every other implicated component of my life, arche, and metron.

14. I pray that every spiritual object, tattoo,

device, label, jewel, necklace, earring, crown, ring, scepter, marker, power source, remote control, tracking device, grid, marking, essence, branding, satanic scroll, Illuminati scroll, super-soldier scroll, New World Order scroll, and all matrixes associated with any and all evil sacred orders placed in and/or around every part of me, my realm, or my sphere of influence to anchor in the group or those in their kingdoms would be consumed in the holy fire of Jesus Christ and totally dissolved. I decree that there cannot be any essence left from the group. I repent for accepting ungodly spirit food and drink and I pray that all ungodly spirit food or drink would be consumed and destroyed from every part of my being. I pray for a deactivation of all related interfaces with my energy field.

15. I now specifically address altars and locations of sacrifice, worship, and dedication that represent me, in and around my home, realm, sphere of influence, or anywhere belonging to the group. I repent on behalf of me (and all my parts) for this idolatry, the spilling of innocent blood, and rituals performed on these altars. Father in heaven, I decree that these altars are now judged and shattered by your lightning in every timeline, age, realm, dimension, frequency, vibration, planet, cosmos, constellation, and universe, past, present, and future, to infinity, and from the beginning across eternity. I decree bankruptcy to all

related evil entities and powers. I specifically repent on behalf of me (and all my parts) for any lust, manipulation, and immorality I engaged in while I was entangled with the group and their kingdoms and involved with their altars. I ask that you restore my innocence, Father God. I request the issuance of restraining orders to the group and anything or anyone else on assignment against me from their kingdom, including backups, from interaction with me, my household, my realm, inheritance, business, timelines, family lines, and bloodlines.

16. I now take authority over every evil entity and every unholy thing on me and/or around me that has been operating under the authority of the group. I declare that you are discovered, apprehended, bound, pierced through, and thrust out of me for judgment. I declare you are being sent to where the True Lord Jesus Christ sends you.

17. I identify every ungodly insertion placed in my timelines, family lines, bloodlines, seasons, and anywhere else by the group. Lord Jesus, I decree that these must now be extracted, consumed, and destroyed. I ask that you replace these with godly events.

18. I call for every algorithm or formula created from my DNA and genetic material that is projected throughout the group to be shut down in every age, realm, dimension, frequency,

vibration, and timeline, past, present and future, to infinity, including all counterfeit and alternate creations. I command the immediate apprehension of all hybrids and every cosmic artificial intelligence and technology behind those projections and call for viruses encoded with heavenly algorithms to be uploaded into them and their computers in order to destroy them in judgment. I curse their computers with a curse of non-existence.

19. I identify every intergalactic and interplanetary data bank and computer that contains within its records or mainframe: data, equations, parts, algorithms, and information of any manner extracted from my humanity. I declare that angels are sent forth to liberate every part of me held captive in these data banks. I pray that all records and information in them related to me would be forcefully erased and permanently deleted. I call for the lightning of God to destroy every ungodly altar (both sacrificial and honorary) as well as effigies contained within the group representing me or bearing my name, image, or likeness, or in me, representing the group and bearing their names, images, or likenesses. I also call for the annulling and removal of every curse and ungodly insertion placed on the times and seasons of my life in synchronicity with the group. I receive synchronization with what has been written about me in the books of the Most High God.

20. I cover and seal the moment of this renunciation along with all godly interventions in all of my timelines with your heavenly gold. I decree it is locked down and blocked from all tampering and resets by heavenly protection. I close every unholy door known and unknown, seen and unseen, and call them completely sealed from this point in time and out of time, forward and backward and in every direction, inside out, upside down, back and forth, reversed, inverted, and vortexed, in Jesus's name. I decree that all theft of energy, life force, or any other godly blessing must be returned a hundredfold. I ask for recompense on behalf of me and all whom I represent. I render this entire confession established in every timeline, age, realm, dimension, frequency, vibration, planet, cosmos, constellation, and universe, past, present, and future, to infinity, and from the beginning across eternity.

21. Lastly, I decree an edict for retaliation: All attempts at retaliation and backlash will be sentenced and judged immediately, up to and including the destruction of all owned territory and trade routes implicated, and the permanent removal of all title, inheritance, status, prestige, calling, and ability in the spirit. Let this be read in every realm, age, dimension, and timeline, that Jesus would have as a warning. I call for this to be posted outside of my sphere and realm. Amen.

PRAYERS REQUIRING ACTIVATION

Now to Him who is able to do exceedingly
abundantly above all that we ask or think,
according to the power that works in us,

to Him be glory in the church by Christ
Jesus to all generations, forever and
ever. Amen.

Ephesians 3:20–21

EVENING PRAYER 2.0

In this final section of the book, you will find what I call prayers requiring activation. These prayers are established upon components of our inheritance in Christ that, until recently, have remained highly unexplored by the body of Christ. These components include the arche (pronounced Ark-EE), star, and mountain. The arche is a magistrate, heavenly jurisdiction and beginning. When it comes to the arche, we have learned that it is a realm that is often locked until Jesus Christ opens it up to the person. We have seen that the arche may be defiled upon discovery and require deliverance and cleansing work. The same thing goes for the star, which exists in the spirit world and can function like a vehicle for our spirit, among other things. Our mountain, which also exists in the spirit, is a place to build and explore with Christ. It is capable of being superimposed on our assignment sphere and establishing spiritual government.

As this book is not a teaching tool, I will simply take this opportunity to refer you to our course called *Realms and Dimensions Unsealed* at www.bridemin-istriesinstitute.com. If you have not taken that course, and gotten your arche, star, and mountain discovered and cleaned up in the spirit, I would not recommend venturing any further into this book. As a prerequisite for this, you will want to have your human spirit fully activated, which is explained in our course called *How to Minister to the Human Spirit*. For those of you that have done this and are ready to step into the next level, this next section is for you. The language in the following prayers will be most effective with a functional human spirit that has received access to its arche, mountain, and star. This requires activation, or one could say, intentional ministry, for most believers.

Having said this, let me introduce this prayer. In the first volume of *Prayers that Shake Heaven and Earth*, I included my Evening Prayer. This was the first prayer that I wrote down and began to share with people. For this reason, it holds a special place in my heart. While that prayer has blessed and changed many lives, I learned over time that there were many people that it was not powerful enough to help. If it did help, the fruit remained limited. For those that need some extra power before going to sleep, I composed a second version. It covers similar territory to the first prayer but adds a host of other elements that are sure to radically shift your environment before laying down your head for sleep.

Father God, I come before you in prayer
to prepare this atmosphere for my rest. I

enter into your gates with thanksgiving and I enter into your courts with praise. I thank you for all that you have done today.

I receive my identity in Christ as a king and I declare that a king sleeps in a fortress that is fortified with guards. Lord Jesus, I claim you as my shield, buckler, rearguard, strong tower, and fortress. Tonight, I appoint angels to stand guard at the north, south, east, and west, as well as above, below, and against every dimensional access point in Jesus's name. I decree that the blood of Jesus covers this place and extends out to the perimeter. I also speak that the blood of Jesus covers everything under my stewardship. I speak that canals of oil of anointing are established around the perimeter and I call them set on fire with holy consuming fire in the name of Jesus!

I put up smoke screens in the spirit acting as sight and sound barriers against satanic agents, interlopers, and evil spirits. I speak that every curse, hex, vex, spell, incantation, voodoo, sorcery, form of witchcraft, dark art, enchantment, smote, or other form of weaponized demonic activity sent against me or my family would be reversed upon the heads of the senders sevenfold that they would know that Jesus is Lord. I attach booby traps and snares to the evil assignments that have been taken out against me and my family, so that as evil entities take those assignments, they are snared and judged while I enjoy sweet, uninterrupted sleep in the name of Jesus. I box spirits in with angels surrounding those boxes that will worship Jesus all night long so that they would know the glory of the name of Jesus. Lord God, I thank you that the military might of heaven, engines of war, and chariots of fire are stationed around the property and that interdimensional entities, witches, and evil agents coming in to harass or cause other issues are confronted, derailed, and introduced to the power of Jesus Christ.

Furthermore, I cancel and render powerless all attempts at mind-to-mind communication, dream manipulation, and all other forms of psychic and telepathic intrusion, in the name of Jesus. I thank you that all of my dreams are inspired by your Holy Spirit. I declare that my sleep will be sweet, uninterrupted, and that upon waking I will be well rested. I also put on the armor of light. I take up the helmet of salvation, the breastplate of righteousness, the belt of truth, I declare that my feet are shod with the preparation of the gospel of peace, and I take up the shield of faith to quench all the fiery darts of the wicked one, and the sword of the Spirit, which is the word of God.

Lord God, I thank you that you are filling my room with the sweet frequency of rest, relaxation, restoration, and recuperation. I thank you that my mind receives your grace and that as I lay my head to sleep there is a stillness and quietness that comes over my person as your angels wrap me up. For it is written that he that dwells in the secret place of the Most High will abide under the shadow of the Almighty. I thank you that there is marshal law instituted upon all parts of my humanity attempting to go out of body and engage in astral traffic and trade that is ungodly and unauthorized. I arm angels with sleeping gas that will put deep sleep upon all compromised parts of my humanity. I thank you that angels are stationed round about the perimeter with the assignment to immediately apprehend and put in the immediate presence of the true Lord Jesus Christ any parts that are attempting to go out-of-body, run, connect with abusers, report to cults or covens, and report to evil entities and powers in the heavens. It is not permitted!

I speak that my arche is established round about this perimeter. I call the arche, and the weaponry of God's angels on assignment, charged with the names of God: Jehovah-Jireh, Jehovah-Rapha, Jehovah-Shammah, Jehovah-Nissi, Jehovah-Tsidkenu, Jehovah-Makkedesh, Jehovah-Ra'ah, Jehovah-Shalom, Jehovah-Gibbowr, Jehovah-Elohim, Jehovah-Sabaoth, Jehovah-Issuwz, Jehovah-Hoseenu, Jehovah-Chayil, Jehovah-Quanna, Jehovah-Milchamah, El-Shaddai, El-Elyon, El-Olam, El-Roy, Yeshuah Ha Mashiach.

I furthermore interface my arche with the seven Spirits of God; the Spirit of the Lord, the Spirit of Wisdom and Understanding, the Spirit of Counsel and Might, the Spirit of Knowledge, and the Fear of the Lord. I invite the Living Letters to come in and vibrate in accordance with their resonate frequencies bringing heaven and earth into alignment. I establish my star as a power core, supercharging my arche through alignment and interface. I also superimpose my mountain and open up trade routes into heavenly places in Christ Jesus, imposing the jurisdiction and government of Zion. I call these matters settled in the name of Jesus. Amen.

MARRIAGE PRAYER

Marriage is something that God considers holy.
Marriage is a covenant that brings two people together
in all that they are and all that they have for the purpose of raising a family, impacting their community,
and establishing kingdom mandates in the heavens
and in the earth. I believe that healthy families are the
foundation of strong communities, and that strong
families begin with strong marriages. Unfortunately,
many marriages struggle and fall apart. Of those that
survive, many are filled with disappointment, wounds,
and strife. If this is your experience with marriage,
my heart truly goes out to you. You aren't alone. As
the author of this book, I too have been through the
tragedy of divorce, and I understand your struggle.

This prayer was written by my wife, Christian.
It has become something we pray together on a reg-
ular basis because it has incredible power that goes
far beyond your typical marriage prayer. It is essen-
tially an entanglement of heavenly inheritances and
earthly resources. This prayer will probably read awk-
wardly, as it employs language that is not common
to the knowledge base of most believers. Therefore,
it has been saved for the end of the book. Ideally, the
husband and wife will both have their spirits fully

activated, as well as their stars, mountains, and arche. When a husband and wife are fully unlocked into these components of their inheritance in Christ and begin to say this prayer, the results will be extraordinary. I should know; my wife and I are walking in the fruit right now!

If you are wondering if you can just jump right in and use the prayer without having these elements activated and cleaned up in the spirit first, the answer is yes. I can't stop you from using any of the prayers in this book at your discretion. However, if your spouse is in heavy demonic bondage or you are already navigating severe abuse situations, this prayer is not likely to be your deliverance. It will simply entwine you deeply with your spouse in their pit of their darkness. This prayer is to bond people together that are mutually seeking Christ and wanting to enjoy the full benefits of their union in the heavens and on the earth. For those that are mutually pursuing Christ and seeking him to be the centerpiece of their marriage relationship, this prayer will take you to new and glorious heights.

> Father God, we come before you in the mighty name of Jesus. We bring our heavenly mansions, arches, metra, stars, mountains, living stones, and trees into alignment along with our bodies, souls,

hearts, and spirits. We connect our businesses and ministries, as well as all other ordained exploits. We call our realms charged with the names of God, Jehovah-Jireh, Jehovah-Rapha, Jehovah-Shammah, Jehovah-Nissi, Jehovah-Tsidkenu, Jehovah-Makkedesh, Jehovah-Ra'ah, Jehovah-Shalom, Jehovah-Gibbowr, Jehovah-Elohim, Jehovah-Sabaoth, Jehovah-Issuwz, Jehovah-Hoseenu, Jehovah-Quana, Jehovah-Chayil, Jehovah-Milchamah, El-Shaddai, El-Elyon, El-Olam, El-Roy, Yeshuah Ha Mashiach.

We furthermore interface our realms with the seven Spirits of God; the Spirit of the Lord, the Spirit of Wisdom and Understanding, the Spirit of Counsel and Might, the Spirit of Knowledge, and the Fear of the Lord. We also invite the Living Letters into our realms in order to vibrate in accordance with their resonant frequencies bringing heaven and earth into alignment.

We declare that what the Lord has put together, let no man put asunder. We open our hearts to receive your thoughts about each other and determine to receive and meditate on what you reveal. We purpose to walk together and in agreement. We open our hearts to receive conviction wherever mistreatment is occurring and refuse to tolerate it within the confines of our union. We receive ongoing revelation that will allow us to love each other, not according to the limits of our humanity, but according to the limitlessness of the love which you put on the inside of us. Thank you, King Jesus, for the unveiling of your vision for our marriage. We receive it as a branding upon our hearts, established by the work of your Holy Spirit. Amen.

REALM BUSTER PRAYER

Raiding dark realms is sometimes necessary in the course of working with people in deep bondage. The foundation for this prayer is discussed at length in our course called *Realms and Dimensions Unsealed* at the BRIDE Ministries Institute. It can be accessed from our institute website found at www.brideministriesinstitute.com.

This prayer is written to be spoken over someone receiving ministry. Use this prayer when you are confronted by regions of captivity, such as prisons in other dimensions, craft, other planets, solar systems, or other regions of the spirit where the person you are working with has aspects of their humanity enslaved. Use introduction "A" to raid a realm that is holding a person in bondage if you are confident that your human spirit has an instrument capable of determining the coordinates of a realm in the spirit. Use introduction "B" to receive the unknown realm's coordinates from Jesus. Use introduction "C" if you or the person you are praying for is already seeing the realm in the spirit where a part of them is being held in captivity. Typically, it will either be fractals of the human spirit or soul-fragments that are being held in captivity. Sometimes it will be their DNA. In the blank you may say, "so-and-so's spirit", or the proper name of an alternate personality (soul-fragment) that you come to realize has been taken out of the body. Introduction "D" can be employed if you are seeing a realm and know what it's called. For example, you may say, "Orion" or "Mars" in the first underlined area if your knowledge is this thorough.

When using this prayer, you will either speak Point 1 or Point 2 in two places. Using the language of Point 1 is specifically for addressing evil or usurped realms. If the realm of captivity is part of God's creation, such as a planet in another galaxy that has been usurped by evil powers, you can pray Point 2, calling for cleansing and healing by living water instead of Point 1, which calls for the realms to be rolled up as scrolls and delivered to the Father for judgment. Use Point 1 whenever you are dealing with an evil realm, a counterfeit timeline, or anything not original to the creation of God. If you don't know what you are dealing with, my advice is to default to Point 1, because at the end of the day, God's judgments are always righteous regarding everything brought before him.

A. Father God, I come before you in the mighty name of Jesus Christ. I engage my finder and pull up the coordinates of the realm in which _____ is being held in bondage.

B. Father God, I come before you in the mighty

name of Jesus Christ. I pray that Jesus would provide the coordinates of the realm in which _____ is being held in bondage.

C. Father God, I come before you in the mighty name of Jesus Christ. I engage with the realm that has been identified as a region of captivity in which _____ is being held in bondage.

D. Father God, I come before you in the mighty name of Jesus Christ. I identify _____ as a region of captivity in which _____ is being held in bondage.

I declare that my arche is engaged and is now overtaking the realm that has been identified. I call my arche charged with the names of God: Jehovah-Jireh, Jehovah-Rapha, Jehovah-Shammah, Jehovah-Nissi, Jehovah-Tsidkenu, Jehovah-Makkedesh, Jehovah-Ra'ah, Jehovah-Shalom, Jehovah-Gibbowr, Jehovah-Elohim, Jehovah-Sabaoth, Jehovah-Issuwz, Jehovah-Hoseenu, Jehovah-Quana, Jehovah-Chayil, Jehovah-Milchamah, El-Shaddai, El-Elyon, El-Olam, El-Roy, Yeshua Ha Mashiach. I furthermore interface my arche with the Seven Spirits of God: The Spirit of the Lord, Wisdom and Understanding, the Spirit of Counsel and Might, the Spirit of Knowledge, and the Fear of the Lord. I invite the Living Letters into my arche in order to vibrate in accordance with their resonant frequencies bringing heaven and earth into alignment. I establish my star as a power core, supercharging my arche through alignment and interface. I also superimpose my mountain and open up trade routes into heavenly places in Christ Jesus, imposing the jurisdiction and government of Zion.

I identify every back door, backup program, power source and backup power source, bomb, trip wire, and booby trap, past, present, and future, to infinity. I cause them to be consumed in the holy fire of Jesus Christ and totally dissolved. I identify every gate, frequency, barrier, equation, cloaking device, force field, sacred geometry, apex of time, DNA matrix, formula, or defensive protocol that would otherwise guard and protect this realm. I ask you, King Jesus, to unlock, set aside, and completely dismiss with these, right now.

I engage with your word in Isaiah 61, which says, "The Spirit of the Lord God is upon Me, Because the Lord has anointed Me to preach good tidings to the poor; He has sent Me to heal the brokenhearted, To proclaim liberty to the captives, And the opening of the prison to those who are bound; To proclaim the acceptable year of the Lord, And the day of vengeance of our God." It is written in John 8:36 that he whom the Son has set free is free indeed. It is written in Isaiah 45:2 that you will break in pieces the gates of brass and cut in two the bars of iron. I open up the windows of heaven and loose the armies of the Lord, warhorses, and chariots of fire. I cause every prison, laboratory, dungeon, and evil facility to be expunged of all human parts, spirit, soul, and body, and that these parts would be exported through a wormhole to third heavenly places for processing.

I call for angels to collect the testimonies of injustice from every part of humanity being collected from out of this realm. I command that these testimonies are taken to the courts of heaven and weighed on the scales of justice. Based on the injustice detailed by these testimonies, I demand judgment. I call for a sevenfold restoration granted for every injustice that is detailed.

I indict the ruling powers overseeing the realm into the courts of heaven. For all human overseers, I release the gospel of Jesus Christ. Jesus Christ is the Son of God and the Creator. He is the firstborn among many brethren. He was born of a virgin, he died for our sins, and was raised again to life on the third day. He has ascended on high, where he is seated at the right hand of the Father and ever lives to make intercession for the saints. He is the payment for our sins, and should you choose him, you will be justified freely by grace through the redemption that is found in him. His suffering will atone for your sins. If you do not choose him, you will receive in your own members the judgment for your sins and impropriety. Choose now.

I pray, Lord God, that as they make their decisions, your stream of living water flows through the courtroom to separate out humanity from those that exist as composite entities. I pray that your sword would sever devices, demons, blinders, artificial intelligence, programs, holographic technologies, quantum interfaces, and other defilements that would otherwise inhibit a decision for Jesus to be made by those present in the court, thus revealing the true conviction of their humanity and not the instruments of their bondage. Lord, I appeal to you to judge and judge justly, and to have your angels escort those that have not chosen Jesus to the place determined for them. I call for grievous labors and brutal affliction to be imposed upon all non-human rulers and that they would be confined to realms of torment in chains of heaviness and bondage in the name of Jesus.

I identify the pillars of this realm and call for their collapse in the name of Jesus. I decree that the foundations are torn up and destroyed. I pray that every cage, castle, dungeon, laboratory, prison, facility, and construct would be raided and expunged of useful technology and information, to be taken to the third heaven for processing and further study. I command that once the realm has been expunged of all value, all evil buildings and structures would be collapsed into a ruinous heap, never to be rebuilt again.

I go after every demon associated with the realm and declare that they will neither escape nor receive job reassignment. I call for the establishment of prisons that are locked with locks that have no key. I call for angels to gather up and bind all demons associated with this realm and lock them into these prisons with chains and fetters of iron. I call for the prisons to be set on fire, electrified with the lightning of God, and cast into the abyss for failed assignment.

I give assignment that all human virtue would be expunged from this realm and purged with living water. I call for it to be returned to those from whom it has been stolen.

1. I call for the realm to be rolled up as a scroll and delivered to the Father for judgment. In its void I command the establishment of a heavenly outpost staffed by warring angels. I call this territory claimed for the kingdom of God and that it will henceforth serve as a kingdom outpost in the heavens.

2. I call for the river of Living Water flowing from the throne of God to now flow through

this realm in order to bring cleansing, healing, and restoration to the original estate in the name of Jesus.

I seal this work in every realm, age, timeline, dimension, frequency, vibration, planet, cosmos, constellation, and universe, past, present, and future, to infinity and from the beginning across eternity.

I now move to multiply the judgment. I declare that realms that are discovered to have engaged in ungodly trade and trafficking with the realm being judged are now being identified and that their coordinates are now being delivered to the armies of heaven. I expand my arche and overtake the coordinates of all of the realms that have been identified. I discover every back door, backup program, power source and backup power source past, present, and future, to infinity. I cause them to be consumed in the holy fire of Jesus Christ and totally dissolved. I identify every gate, frequency, barrier, equation, cloaking device, force field, sacred geometry, DNA matrix, or defensive protocol that would otherwise guard and protect these realms. I ask you, King Jesus, to unlock, set aside, and completely dismiss with these, right now.

I cause every cage, castle, prison, laboratory, dungeon, and evil facility in these realms to be expunged of all human parts, spirit, soul, and body, and that these parts would be exported through wormholes to third heavenly places for processing.

I call for angels to collect the testimonies of injustice from every part of humanity being collected from these realms. I command that these testimonies are taken to the courts of heaven and weighed on the scales of justice. Based on the injustice detailed by these testimonies, I demand judgment. I call for the plundering and punishment of these realms, and that they would be judged by the mallet of justice and your rod of iron.

I indict the ruling powers overseeing these realms into the courts of heaven. I decree that they must be forced to give an account for wrongs committed and suffer the judgment deserved by their actions. For all human overseers, I release the gospel of Jesus Christ. Jesus Christ is the Son of God and the Creator. He is the firstborn among many brethren. He was born of a virgin, he died for our sins, and was raised again to life on the third day. He has ascended on high where he is seated at the right hand of the Father and ever lives to make intercession for the saints. He is the payment for our sins, and should you choose him, you will be justified freely by grace through the redemption that is found in him. His suffering will atone for your sins. If you do not choose him, you will receive in your own members the judgment for your sins and impropriety. Choose now.

I pray, Lord God, that as they make their decisions, your stream of living water flows through the courtroom to separate out humanity from those that exist as composite entities. I pray that your sword would sever devices, demons, blinders, artificial intelligence, programs, holographic technologies, quantum interfaces, and other defilements that would otherwise inhibit a decision for Jesus to be made by those present in the court, thus revealing the true conviction of their humanity and not the instruments of their bondage. Lord, I appeal to you to judge and judge justly, and to have your angels escort those that have not chosen Jesus to the place determined for them. I call for grievous labors and brutal affliction to be imposed upon all non-human rulers and that they would be confined to realms of torment in chains of heaviness and bondage in the name of Jesus.

I go after every demon associated with these realms and declare that they will neither escape nor receive job reassignment. I call for the establishment of prisons that are locked with locks that have no key. I call for angels to gather up and bind all demons associated with these realms and lock them into these prisons with chains and fetters of iron. I call for the prisons to be set on fire, electrified with the lightning of God, and cast into the abyss for failed assignment.

I give assignment that all human virtue would be expunged from these realms and purged with living water. I call for it to be returned to those from whom it has been stolen.

1. I call for the realms to be rolled up as scrolls and delivered to the Father for judgment. In their voids I command the establishment of a heavenly outposts staffed by warring angels. I call these territories claimed for the kingdom of God that they will henceforth serve as kingdom outposts in the heavens.

2. I call for the river of Living Water flowing from the throne of God to now flow through these realms in order to bring cleansing, healing, and restoration to the original estate in the name of Jesus.

I seal this work in every realm, age, timeline, dimension, frequency, vibration, planet, cosmos, constellation, and universe, past, present, and future, to infinity and from the beginning across eternity. Amen.

CORRECTION OF FORMULAS
AND EQUATIONS

This prayer is a bit difficult to explain. Most of us can agree that God upholds all things by the Word of his power (Hebrews 1:3). Taking this a few steps further, we learn that Jesus is the Alpha and the Omega, which are the first and last letters of the Greek alphabet. This means that Jesus, who is Jewish, is actually the Aleph Tav, the first and last letters of the Hebrew alphabet. The Hebrew alphabet, for those who are studied, is more than just a collection of letters. It is an incredibly complex algorithm, particularly when we talk about the Paleo-Hebrew. From the algorithm of language, formulas and equations are derived which define the operational parameters for everything in the creation, including you and me.

As we explore the word of God, we learn that God's word is living and powerful. This means that the language contains life, which comes from the letters of the original Hebrew. We have learned that the original Hebrew letters are living beings found in Christ Jesus. For this reason, we refer to them as Living Letters. What we have found, however, is that through the use of evil and counterfeit Living Letters, the formulas and equations that encode our existence have been manipulated and defiled. This prayer calls for a correction of this deep issue, which is afflicting our nature at the sub-quantum level.

In my experience, people often feel subtle, deep shifts with mild to moderate physiological responses as they go through this prayer. However, the testimonies that have resulted from this prayer have extraordinary significance. This prayer is worded to be prayed over oneself or another person. Simply put the words "me/my" into the underlined areas **or** the name of the person you are praying over. This prayer, like the others, should only be prayed once the prayer worker's spirit, arche, mountain, and star are thoroughly activated.

> King Jesus, I invite your presence to surround and overtake _____ down and into his/her/my sub-quantum components.
>
> I engage with my arche and call it charged with the names of God: Jehovah-Jireh, Jehovah-Rapha, Jehovah-Shammah, Jehovah-Nissi, Jehovah-Tsidkenu, Jehovah-Makkedesh, Jehovah-Ra'ah, Jehovah-Shalom, Jehovah-Gibbowr, Jehovah-Elohim, Jehovah-Sabaoth, Jehovah-Issuwz, Jehovah-Hoseenu, Jehovah-Quana, Jehovah-Chayil,

Jehovah-Milchamah, El-Shaddai, El-Elyon, El-Olam, El-Roy, Yeshua Ha Mashiach.

I furthermore interface my arche with the Seven Spirits of God: The Spirit of the Lord, Wisdom and Understanding, the Spirit of Counsel and Might, the Spirit of Knowledge, and the Fear of the Lord. I invite the Living Letters into my arche in order to vibrate in accordance with their resonant frequencies bringing heaven and earth in alignment. I establish my star as a power core, supercharging my arche through alignment and interface. I also superimpose my mountain and open up trade routes into heavenly places in Christ Jesus, imposing the jurisdiction and government of Zion.

I establish my arche round about _____ and identify the formulas and equations governing the parameters of operation of his/her/my body, soul, heart, spirit, and all other components related to livelihood that have been targeted by evil agendas. I identify formulas and equations that have been manipulated into an unbalanced or defiled form, formulas and equations that have had ungodly additions and subtractions made to them, and godly formulas and equations that have been stolen. I declare that all artificial protection of hijacked formulas and equations must now be unlocked and dismissed, inclusive of all gates, frequencies, barriers, evil equations, cloaking devices, force fields, sacred geometries, DNA matrixes, apexes of time, evil formulas, and defensive protocols. I call all formula and algorithmic-based passwords hacked and overridden by heavenly viruses granting unrestricted access to the redemptive power of God right now.

I pray for the release of golden rain in order to wash over and balance every godly equation and to minister to every godly formula. I call for the evidence found in the heavenly cosmic records that details the injustice endured as a result of manipulated formulas and equations to be presented now and weighed on the scales of justice. I command that all counterfeit mathematical characters and counterfeit living letters are now indicted into the courts of heaven to give an account for wrongs committed and suffer the judgment deserved by their actions. I call for the deletion of ungodly formulas and equations at this time. I also pray for the simultaneous restoration of godly formulas and equations that have been stolen. I speak that there is a de-interfacing of formulas and equations with evil computers and I call for an interfacing with the perfect and golden formulas and equations of Jesus Christ. In this I call for the removal of all implicated evil quantum structures and artificial intelligences of every type. I declare that programs that have been written into evil formulas and equations allowing for their infinite reconstitution must now be deleted forever.

I pray that all foundations would be moved from the former formulas and equations and settled upon the formulas and equations that have been corrected by Jesus Christ. I claim you, Jesus Christ, as the chief cornerstone and the rock and foundation. I call for the sealing of the corrected formulas and equations in a safe of heavenly gold acting as a Faraday cage, protecting against all wave and frequency-based attacks. I call this entire work sealed in every realm, age, timeline, dimension, frequency, vibration, planet, cosmos, constellation, and universe, past, present, and future, to infinity, and from the beginning across eternity. Amen.

DELIVERANCE FROM
EVIL TIMELINES

Collapsing evil timelines is required for almost every human on the planet. As with the other prayers in this section, this type of prayer should not be attempted until your human spirit is fully functional and has had its arche, star, and mountain activated into use. The basic idea is that God has books that he has written about us, detailing the many things that he has planned for us to do. This is revealed in passages like Psalms 139:16 and Ephesians 2:10. God pre-planned the things he wants us to walk in, and they are revealed in godly timelines.

To combat this, the enemy has locked many people into ungodly timelines. He has derailed people through abuse, addiction, anger, violence, self-sabotage, fear, and a host of other tactics that have kept us out of the timelines that reveal God's purpose for our lives. For this reason, by targeting the evil timelines that the enemy has constructed to enslave us, it becomes possible to minister massive shifts into the lives of people. When the evil timelines themselves are judged and destroyed, people are liberated to step back into things that God has for them.

This prayer is written to be prayed over another person in a ministry setting. With just slight tweaking, this prayer could easily be prayed over an entire group. Watch and see what the Lord will do!

I begin by engaging with my arche. I call my arche charged with the names of God: Jehovah-Jireh, Jehovah-Rapha, Jehovah-Shammah, Jehovah-Nissi, Jehovah-Tsidkenu, Jehovah-Makkedesh, Jehovah-Ra'ah, Jehovah-Shalom, Jehovah-Gibbowr, Jehovah-Elohim, Jehovah-Sabaoth, Jehovah-Issuwz, Jehovah-Hoseenu, Jehovah-Quana, Jehovah-Chayil, Jehovah-Milchamah, El-Shaddai, El-Elyon, El-Olam, El-Roy, Yeshua Ha Mashiach. I furthermore interface my arche with the Seven Spirits of God: The Spirit of the Lord, Wisdom and Understanding, the Spirit of Counsel and Might, the Spirit of Knowledge, and the Fear of the Lord. I invite the Living Letters into my arche in order to vibrate in accordance with their resonant frequencies bringing heaven and earth in alignment. I establish my star as a power core, supercharging my arche through alignment and interface. I also superimpose my mountain and open up trade routes into heavenly places in Christ Jesus, imposing the jurisdiction and government of Zion.

I now send my arche into the substructure of every evil timeline, time wheel, and time loop where _____'s humanity is being held hostage. I begin by shutting down all types of replication, including replication of evil timelines, time wheels, or time loops, replication of parts, and replication of spoken words.

I go after every computer involved in the replication of evil timelines, time wheels, and time loops in every realm, age, timeline, dimension, frequency, vibration, planet, cosmos, constellation, and universe, past, present and future, to infinity and from the beginning across eternity. I call them uploaded with viruses containing heavenly algorithms and infected beyond repair, taking down and capturing all of their programs and backup programs. I speak that their power sources and backup power sources are targeted with holy fire and entirely consumed and destroyed. I release upon their facilities hailstones, hyper-focused light of God, the broom of destruction, lightning, and the armies of heaven, along with locusts to devour their evil plots. I speak that these computers must be left a ruinous heap never to be rebuilt again.

I loose angels to go after every part of _____'s humanity that is in the possession of the powers of darkness to be replicated by any type of process, along with all existing clones, copies, merfolk, holograms, duplicates, replicas, derivatives, images, or anything else from which a backup of his/her humanity can be assembled and engaged in order to reinstate his/her bondage. I call the timelines, time wheels, and time loops being addressed entirely expunged and that all parts collected are taken to third heavenly places for processing right now in the name of Jesus.

I identify every evil spoken word by members of the family, friends, leaders, and other individuals that have created matter and connected to _____'s DNA. I renounce the counterfeit futures that have been spoken into existence during all rituals, ceremonies, rites of passage, technological processes, or events that have established a counterfeit future and declare that these futures are being held accountable to that which you have written in your books about _____, Lord God. It is written in Matthew 4:4 that man shall not live by bread alone, but by every word that proceeds forth from the mouth of God. It is also written in Matthew 12:36 that for every idle word that men may speak, they will give an account of it in the day of judgment, and so I indict the persons that spoke these idle words into the courts of heaven to give an account for wrongs committed and receive your judgment. I speak that in this accountability, the evil spoken words must be judged and expunged from every earth, timeline, age, realm, dimension, frequency, vibration, planet, cosmos, constellation, and universe, past, present, and future, to infinity, and from the beginning across eternity, ensuring that no backup or reengagement spoken word or related protocol will be able to engage upon the conclusion of this redemptive work.

I now surround every timeline, time wheel, and time loop being addressed with my arche and I identify every back door, backup program, power source and backup power source, bomb, trip wire, and booby trap, past, present, and future, to infinity and from beginning across eternity. I cause them to be consumed in the holy fire of Jesus Christ and totally dissolved. I identify every gate, frequency, barrier, equation, cloaking device, force field, sacred geometry, DNA matrix, apex of time, formula, or defensive protocol that would otherwise guard and protect these timelines, time wheels, and time loops. I ask you, King Jesus, to unlock, set aside, and completely dismiss with these, right now.

I engage with your word in Isaiah 61, which says, "The Spirit of the Lord God is upon Me, Because the Lord has anointed Me to preach good tidings to the poor; He has sent Me to heal the brokenhearted, To proclaim liberty to the captives, And the opening of the prison to those who are bound; To proclaim the acceptable year of the Lord, And the day of vengeance of our God". It is written in John 8:36 that he whom the Son has set free is free indeed. It is written in Isaiah 45:2 that you will break in pieces the gates of brass and cut in two the bars of iron. I open the windows of heaven and loose the armies of the Lord, warhorses, and chariots of fire. I cause every prison, laboratory, dungeon, and evil facility to be expunged of all human parts, spirit, soul, and body, and that these parts would be exported through wormholes to third heavenly places for processing.

I call for angels to collect the testimonies of injustice from every part of humanity being collected from out of these timelines, time wheels, or time loops. I command that these testimonies are taken to the courts of heaven and weighed on the scales of justice. Based on the injustice detailed by these testimonies, I demand judgment. I call for a sevenfold restoration granted for every injustice that is detailed. I indict the ruling powers overseeing these timelines, time wheels, and time loops into the courts of heaven. I decree that they must be forced to give an account for wrongs committed and suffer the judgment deserved by their actions. For all human overseers, I release the gospel of Jesus Christ. Jesus Christ is the Son of God and the Creator. He is the firstborn among many brethren. He was born of a virgin, he died for our sins, and was raised again to life on the third day. He has ascended on high, where he is seated at the right hand of the Father and ever lives to make intercession for the saints. He is the payment for our sins, and should you choose him, you will be justified freely by grace through the redemption that is found in him. His suffering will atone for your sins. If you do not choose him, you will receive in your own members the judgment for your sins and impropriety. Choose now.

I pray, Lord God, that as they make their decisions, your stream of living water flows through the courtroom to separate out humanity from those that exist as composite entities. I pray that your sword would sever devices, demons, blinders, artificial intelligence, programs, holographic technologies, quantum interfaces, and other defilements that would otherwise inhibit a decision for Jesus to be made by those present in the court, thus revealing the true conviction of their humanity and not the instruments of their bondage. Lord, I appeal to you to judge and judge justly, and to have your angels escort those that have not chosen Jesus to the place determined for them, such that they cannot any longer take or receive assignments against _____

to destroy his/her life and deviate him/her from his/her heavenly mandates. I call for grievous labors and brutal affliction to be imposed upon all non-human rulers and that they would be confined to realms of torment in chains of heaviness and bondage in the name of Jesus.

I identify the pillars of these timelines, time wheels, and time loops and call for their collapse in the name of Jesus. I decree that the foundations are torn up and destroyed. I pray that every cage, castle, dungeon, laboratory, prison, facility, and construct would be raided and expunged of useful technology and information, to be taken to the third heaven for processing and further study. I command that once the timelines, time wheels, and time loops have been expunged of all value, all evil buildings and structures would be collapsed into a ruinous heap, never to be rebuilt again.

I go after every demon associated with these timelines, time wheels, and time loops, and declare that they will neither escape nor receive job reassignment. I call for the establishment of prisons that are locked with locks that have no key. I call for angels to gather up and bind all demons associated with these timelines, time wheels, and time loops, and lock them into these prisons with chains and fetters of iron. I call for the prisons to be set on fire, electrified with the lightning of God, and cast into the abyss for failed assignment.

I give assignment that all human virtue would be expunged from these timelines, time wheels, and time loops and purged with living water. I call for it to be returned to those from whom it has been stolen.

I call for the timelines, time wheels, and time loops to be rolled up as scrolls and delivered to the Father for judgment. In their void, I command the establishment of heavenly outposts staffed by warring angels. I call these territories claimed for the kingdom of God and that they will henceforth serve as kingdom outposts in the heavens. I furthermore call all works in the earth that were plugged into these timelines, time wheels, and time loops expired, ruined, and forever taken out of the way in the name of Jesus.

I seal this work in every realm, age, timeline, dimension, frequency, vibration, planet, cosmos, constellation, and universe, past, present, and future, to infinity and from the beginning across eternity. Amen.

DELIVERANCE OF STARS

I saved this prayer for last. It is designed to be deployed during ministry to unlock and activate a person's star. Unfortunately, the revelation that our inheritance in Christ includes stars that our human spirits will interact with is not common knowledge. I know that until Jesus introduced me to my star, this entire realm of revelation was closed to my understanding as well. As the Church moves into the coming years, this will change. At BRIDE Ministries, we have pioneered in the ministry of getting people's human spirits activated. In the process, God has shown us a step-by-step process for reconnecting people's human spirits to their stars. This has been very exciting.

Alas, like anything, there's always more to the story. I have found it necessary to get stars set free from evil entities lording over them. Isn't it just like the devil to put things in bondage that we don't even know exist?

This prayer is written for use by a person that has been activated to be able to leverage their star, mountain, and their arche in their prayer work. The typical route that one would take before deploying this prayer would be to engage with the spirit of the person they are praying for and pull that spirit to the surface. Then, they would have the spirit escorted by the angels or Jesus to the person's star in the heavens. Once the person's spirit arrives at their star and begins to perceive it, the question will be asked, "Is the star in bondage to an overlord?" If the answer is yes, this prayer should then be deployed.

This prayer is for the advanced prayer minister. Do not fret if the description of this prayer doesn't make sense to you! As I have already explained that this book is a collection of tools and not teachings, I will simply point you to the BRIDE Ministries Institute, where the subject of stars is covered as part of the course called *Realms and Dimensions Unsealed.* We must keep in mind that the things which God has prepared for us are exceedingly abundantly above anything we can ask, think, or imagine. Things are very exciting when we tap into this realm of operation. Having said that, when you need it, this resource will be waiting for you!

> Father God, I come before you in the mighty name of Jesus Christ. I identify the coordinates of this person's star and the entity lording over it, overtaking these things with my arche. I call my arche charged with the names of God: Jehovah-Jireh, Jehovah-Rapha, Jehovah-Shammah, Jehovah-Nissi, Jehovah-Tsidkenu,

Jehovah-Makkedesh, Jehovah-Ra'ah, Jehovah-Shalom, Jehovah-Gibbowr, Jehovah-Elohim, Jehovah-Sabaoth, Jehovah-Issuwz, Jehovah-Hoseenu, Jehovah-Quana, Jehovah-Chayil, Jehovah-Milchamah, El-Shaddai, El-Elyon, El-Olam, El-Roy, Yeshua Ha Mashiach.

I furthermore interface my arche with the Seven Spirits of God: The Spirit of the Lord, Wisdom and Understanding, the Spirit of Counsel and Might, the Spirit of Knowledge, and the Fear of the Lord. I invite the Living Letters into my arche in order to vibrate in accordance with their resonant frequencies bringing heaven and earth in alignment. I establish my star as a power core, supercharging my arche through alignment and interface. I also superimpose my mountain and open up trade routes into heavenly places in Christ Jesus, imposing the jurisdiction and government of Zion.

I call for the heavenly cosmic records to be pulled up and for the record of injustices performed by the evil entity lording over this star to be extracted and detailed. I furthermore declare that upon the reading of these injustices, every gate, barrier, frequency, equation, cloaking device, force field, sacred geometry, DNA matrix, apex of time, formula, or defensive protocol that would otherwise guard or protect human fragments, spirit, soul, or body held by the entity in its person, breastplate, clothing, crown, scepter, throne, or anything else under its jurisdiction are collapsed and moved out of the way. It is written in John 8:36 that he whom the Son has set free is free indeed. It is written in Isaiah 45:2 that you will break in pieces the gates of brass and cut in two the bars of iron.

I speak that all human parts are collected to third heavenly places for processing and that their testimonies of injustice are presented before the courts of heaven and weighed on the scales of justice. On the basis of the witness against the evil entity, I volley against it weapons of warfare. I release lightning, hailstones, tsunamis of living water, the east winds of judgment, the plague, confusion, fear of the day and fear of the night, the hiss of the Lord that brings the bees and flies, ravenous beasts, the broom of destruction, the threshing sledge, the warhorses of heaven and chariots of fire.

I declare that the entity and its underlings are dislodged and that their power over this star, and over all other hijacked stars, is now being taken away by force as judgment is rendered. I speak that its scepter, crown, throne, and other elements of influence and lordship are shattered by the power of the blood of Jesus and I call this star set free.

I furthermore move to identify the cords plugging this star into evil agendas, facilities, strongholds, laboratories, and realms, in the heavens and on the earth. I call the cords severed along with all of their backup programs to infinity and end the powering up of evil agendas with this star. I furthermore call for the river of living water flowing from the throne of God to run through this star in order to cleanse it, redeem it, and restore it to its first estate. I also call for the bread of life to be delivered and ministered to the star and that it would be baptized in the fire of Jesus Christ. Thank you, Lord Jesus, for setting this star free. Amen.